EJACULATE RESPONSIBLY

A WHOLE NEW WAY TO THINK ABOUT ABORTION

EJACULATE RESPONSIBLY
A WHOLE NEW WAY TO THINK ABOUT ABORTION

GABRIELLE BLAIR

WORKMAN PUBLISHING • NEW YORK

Library of Congress Cataloging-in-Publication Data is available

ISBN 978-1-5235-2318-4

Design by Bonnie Siegler

Workman books are available at special discounts when purchased in bulk
for premiums and sales promotions as well as for fundraising or educational
use. Special editions or book excerpts can also be created to specification.
For details, please contact specialmarkets@hbgusa.com.

Workman Publishing Co., Inc., a subsidiary of Hachette Book Group, Inc.
1290 Avenue of the Americas
New York, NY 10104
workman.com

WORKMAN is a registered trademark of Workman Publishing Co., Inc.,
a subsidiary of Hachette Book Group, Inc.

Printed in the United States of America on responsibly sourced paper.
First printing September 2022

10 9 8 7 6 5 4 3 2 1

*To the people of the future
who get to live their lives with no anxiety
about unwanted pregnancies,
and to the responsible ejaculators
who I'm confident can and will make that possible.*

a crucial refocus:
IT'S THE MEN.

Dear Reader, before we begin, I'm going to make a quick introduction, and a short, sincere plea.

I'm a religious mother of six, who accidentally made a career as a thought leader after I started a blog, Design Mom, in 2006, and it took off. I've received accolades I'm proud of—my blog was named a Website of the Year by *Time* magazine, it won the Iris Award for Blog of the Year, and I've written a *New York Times* bestselling book (also called *Design Mom*). I've moderated hundreds of discussions on difficult topics and interviewed some of the most influential people in the world. My writing is quoted and shared across the globe daily. And the most important essay I've ever written, an essay about abortion, is what this book is based on.

In that essay, I proposed several ideas about the often-overlooked causes of abortion. My key claim is that 99 percent of abortions are the result of unwanted pregnancies, and men cause all unwanted pregnancies. Currently, conversations about abortion are entirely centered on women—on women's bodies, and whether women have a right to terminate an unwanted pregnancy. For those who want to effectively reduce abortion (or outlaw it altogether, as many states have done), this focus on women is a fundamental mistake for two reasons: 1) because there is clear data that abortion bans are ineffective and 2) because, again, *men* cause all unwanted pregnancies. If you're focused on women, you're wasting your time.

Don't believe me that men cause all unwanted pregnancies? Let me walk you through it. I've got twenty-eight simple arguments in this book explaining how and why this is true.

An unwanted pregnancy doesn't happen because people have sex. An unwanted pregnancy only happens if a man ejaculates irresponsibly—if he deposits his sperm in a vagina when he and his partner are not trying to conceive. It's not asking a lot for men to avoid this.

We've put the burden of pregnancy prevention on the person who is fertile for 24 hours a month, instead of the person who is fertile 24 hours a day, every day of their life.

I don't know what your thoughts are on abortion, but you picked up this book, so I assume you care about it—as a right to fight for or a problem to solve. Whatever your feelings and beliefs are on abortion, I'm going to ask that you momentarily set them to the side. I'll do the same (though anyone really curious about where I stand can google me). Why set them aside? Because the arguments I lay out in this book are an attempt to shift the conversation away from the usual for-or-against debates that have stymied this issue for decades. I'm going to present a new approach that I hope you'll find refreshing and productive.

My sincere gratitude for being open to a new way of thinking,

Gabrielle Blair

A NOTE ON LANGUAGE

I want to let you know right from the get go that the arguments I'm presenting are written from a cisgender heterosexual perspective. While I welcome all readers and I hope everyone learns something from my arguments, applying LGBTQIA+-inclusive language to my arguments would only serve to erase the singular experiences of queer, trans, and nonbinary people, whether they are people who produce sperm or people who can become pregnant. Ultimately, I make a cisgender heterosexual argument for people engaging in cisgender heterosexual sexual relationships (say that ten times fast).

It's important to make that clear so that you can manage your expectations before you begin, but also because I want everyone to feel comfortable here. Yes, it's a cisgender heterosexual perspective, but perhaps you'll find descriptions in these pages, about things like power dynamics and responsibilities, that can serve all perspectives.

While we're on the topic of language, two vocabulary notes: When I use the word *ejaculate*, I'm referring to ejaculation that releases semen. When I use the word *abortion*, I'm referring to elective abortions due to unwanted pregnancies, which make up approximately 99 percent of all abortions. I am not referring to the abortions of intended pregnancies as a consequence of health issues for the developing fetus or the mother. Additionally, I want to acknowledge that while I fully understand some people experience temporary or permanent infertility, the arguments in this book are assuming full fertility for both men and women.

THE

ARGUMENTS

MEN ARE 50 TIMES MORE FERTILE THAN WOMEN.

It starts with biology. A woman's body produces a fertile egg for approximately 24 hours each month, from puberty until menopause, which is about thirty-five to forty years. Since the 24 hours might start midday on a Monday and end midday on a Tuesday, we like to say the egg is fertile for two days, but really it's about 24 hours.

A man's sperm is fertile every single second of every single day. And though we know his sperm gets crappier as he ages, a man can produce sperm until the day he dies.

At eighty years old, a woman who menstruated for forty years will have experienced 480 days of fertility.

At eighty years old, a man who hit puberty at age twelve will have experienced 24,208 days of fertility.

So let's do the math. 24,208 divided by 480 . . . carry the 4 . . . and it turns out that compared to women, men have a little more than fifty times the number of fertile days.

Most times when a woman has sex, she cannot be impregnated because her egg is not fertile. Every time a man has sex, he can potentially impregnate someone, because he is always fertile. In theory, in any given year, a fertile man could impregnate a different fertile woman (or more than one!) every single day and cause 365 (or more!) pregnancies. During that same year, a woman can only experience a full pregnancy once.

This enormous disparity in fertility is important to recognize at the outset. I'm not trying to overdramatize this—it's a simple fact of biology. But it points to the reality that men and women are not two equally matched parties when it comes to fertility and potential to cause a pregnancy. One party is more fertile by orders of magnitude.

This fundamental biological reality, up to now rarely mentioned in discussions about unwanted pregnancies and abortion, is actually the heart of the issue. It colors all other arguments.

Once we recognize this disparity in fertility, it becomes crystal clear that pregnancy and abortion are not "a woman's issue." Men don't play a minor or supporting role in pregnancy. Men's lifelong continual fertility is the central driving force behind all unwanted pregnancies.

SPERM
LIVE FOR UP TO
5
DAYS.

A woman who experiences "normal" fertility produces one egg approximately every four weeks. That one egg, or ovum, has a "fertile window" of approximately 12 to 24 hours. Given how narrow this window is, pregnancy should be a pretty easy thing to avoid, right?

Turns out it's not that easy.

For one, sperm live longer than an egg. Once deposited in a woman's body, sperm have a "fertile window" that is up to five days long.

Let's say a man and woman have sex on a Monday. He puts his sperm in her vagina, and then some of the sperm end up sticking around. The man and woman then travel for work in different cities and don't see each other again for a week.

On Monday, the woman's egg isn't fertile and the sperm, which are still hanging out, can't fertilize it.

On Tuesday, her egg isn't fertile, and the sperm can't fertilize it.

On Wednesday, her egg isn't fertile, and the sperm can't fertilize it.

On Thursday, something changes. The woman's egg reaches the fertile point, and the sperm that are still hanging around her vagina suddenly find that they can breach the egg wall, which was impregnable just hours before.

On Thursday, the woman is impregnated via sex that she had on Monday.

So, it's accurate to say that a woman's egg is only fertile for 24 hours every month. But in reality, to avoid a pregnancy, sperm needs to be kept away from an egg for the woman's 24-hour fertility window, plus five days beforehand. To be extra safe, doctors recommend keeping sperm away from eggs for seven days before the 24-hour fertility window.

That seems pretty straightforward: Keep sperm away from eggs for one week each month. Doable. Clear cut. Except for one big problem: Women don't know when their egg is going to be fertile.

WOMEN'S FERTILITY IS UN-PREDICT-ABLE.

There is no neon light that flashes to let a woman know her egg is ready to be fertilized. No alarm clock goes off. No built-in gauge pops when she's fertile, like a turkey timer on Thanksgiving.

There are ways to *estimate* fertility—things like temperature changes, the feel of the lubrication her cervix produces, or breast tenderness. A woman with sore breasts may indeed be ovulating. She might be. Maybe. Possibly.

Some women have menstrual cycles that seem to be as precise as clockwork, and they can use this reliable cycle to *estimate* when they are fertile. Typical medical guidance is that ovulation happens fourteen days after your last period begins, but data doesn't actually back that up, because even the most reliable menstrual cycles are subject to change. A woman may indeed be ovulating fourteen days after her last period starts. She might be. Maybe. Possibly.

All the physical signs and rhythms and cycle tracking amount to nothing if your body can change without warning, which is something that all bodies tend to do. You can try to read the physical signs, and use an app to track changes, but you'll never be totally certain that you've got it right.

You might be thinking: That can't be accurate. It can't be *that* hard to predict when a women will be ovulating. Oh, but it is. Let's look at a 2020 study of 32,595 women published in the scientific journal *Human Reproduction Open*. The purpose of the research was to study the varying lengths of menstrual cycles and to discover when ovulation actually happens.

Boy oh boy, the results were surprising—even among women who *wanted* to be impregnated, and were *trying hard to track their fertility*, using the fourteen-day ovulation guidance was not accurate. Some of the discoveries:

- 31 percent of the women in the study believed their cycle was 28 days, but only 12 percent of them had an actual 28-day cycle.

- 87 percent of the women had menstrual cycle lengths between 23 and 35 days.

- Over half the women (52 percent) had cycles that varied by 5 days or more.

- For those women who did have a 28-day cycle, there was a 10-day spread of ovulation, and the same was true for all the different cycle lengths they studied.

The study concludes:

Even if cycle length can be predicted, the day of ovulation can be very variable, meaning that you cannot accurately predict the fertile phase using cycle length alone.

Although the average length of a woman's menstrual cycle is twenty-eight days, there is considerable . . . variation in cycle lengths as well as changes in a woman's own personal cycle with time. [The] timing of the fertile window is also likely to be highly variable.

The insights gained from these findings highlight the uniqueness of women's menstrual cycles.

The study also spoke directly about what this means when women use apps to try and track fertility:

Apps to track fertility are increasingly being used among women who are seeking to conceive, and many purport to predict ovulation based on cycle length characteristics alone, which can have extremely low predictive accuracy. These apps also assume each woman's fertile window is the same length, disregarding evidence that the length of the fertile window differs among women.

Ultimately, trying to track a woman's fertility by watching the calendar or watching for physical signs, or using an app, is not a tenable form of birth control. It's a risky endeavor, fraught with the biggest possible consequences.

Fertility tests do exist, but they don't solve that pesky "five-day sperm fertility window" issue. The tests tell you whether ovulation is imminent at the moment you test. But they don't tell you if you'll be ovulating next week, or in a few days.

These fertility tests are designed for people who are *trying* for pregnancy; they are not designed, nor are they at all practical, for people trying to keep sperm away from the egg during the fertility window. If the test is positive and you're trying for pregnancy, it means: *Have sex right now! You're about to ovulate, and you can have the sperm ready and waiting in your vagina!*

If you're trying to avoid pregnancy, and the fertility test is positive, that means: *Shoot! I sure hope you didn't have sex for the last five days, and definitely don't have sex for the next few days, too.* Not as helpful.

The idea of using fertility tests as birth control may sound appealing—it's just 12 to 24 hours of fertility, right?—but in practice, women would have to test many days each month to get a really accurate result, and they still wouldn't solve the five-day sperm longevity issue. Plus, these tests won't help for planning ahead—they don't predict whether you'll be ovulating on your honeymoon that takes place next month. As one fertility doctor I spoke with said, "Tracking signs of fertility is really good if you're *trying* to get pregnant, but because ovulation can skip or delay without giving you external signs to track, it's not good at preventing pregnancy and is ABSOLUTELY not recommended to be used as birth control."

Still don't believe that a woman's fertility window is that hard to gauge? Feel free to talk to women who have gone through a dozen rounds of IUI (artificial insemination) at an average cost of $1,300 for each attempt.

We're left to conclude that tracking a woman's fertility is complicated and often inaccurate. And yet, because we're so focused on women's bodies, we put a lot of energy into figuring out when that 24-hour period of egg fertility is going to happen.

At the same time, we ignore the fact of men's fertility. We don't track men's fertility at all. There are no apps for that. No over-the-counter tests at the pharmacy. Because there's no need; we already know when men are fertile. Men are fertile all day, every day.

We have an entire pregnancy prevention industry built around the brief, elusive period of monthly female fertility, and nothing, absolutely nothing even close to equivalent, that addresses the always persistent male fertility. We are laser-focused on the wrong thing.

I'm trying to come up with an analogy for just how non-sensical this is: Imagine you have a couple of neighborhood vandals who are harassing your property. One of them leaves a bag of dog poop on your porch in the middle of the night, every night. So when you wake up and go outside, every single morning there's always a bag of dog poop on your porch. It's gross. It smells horrible. And it's relentless. Sometimes you forget it's there and you accidentally step on the bag and get dog poop on your shoe. And every day you have to pick up the bag and throw it away.

Now imagine there's a second vandal who leaves a bag of rotten food on your porch once a month. It's unpredictable—you never know exactly when they will show up, but it happens once every month. It's also gross and smelly. And you have to dispose of it.

In this scenario, your biggest problem is the nightly poop guy. Sure, you'd like to stop the rotten food guy as well, but the poop guy is relentless. He comes every single night. Solving the poop guy problem would lead to the biggest relief.

In this analogy, what would we say about the property owner who responds to the vandals by all but ignoring the poop guy and instead fastidiously working to figure out exactly when the rotten food guy will show up each month? (*Last month he showed up at midnight on the 13th, and two months ago, he showed up at 6 a.m. on the 14th. So maybe this month, he'll come on the 15th? But then again, three months ago, he came on the 5th. Hmmm. I'm not yet seeing a pattern, but I'm sure I can figure this out.*) We would say that's a ridiculous response.

I know it's not a perfect analogy, but I think it helps point out that our focus on women's fertility, instead of men's fertility, is misplaced when it comes to pregnancy prevention.

We treat ejaculation as something that happens at random, that is unintentional, that is impossible to anticipate or predict.

And we treat ovulation like it can be pinpointed well in advance and easily predicted.

Somehow, we've confused the two.

OVULATION IS INVOLUNTARY, EJACULATION IS NOT.

Women cannot control when they are fertile. Women cannot choose when ovulation begins or ends. Women cannot control the movement of their egg. During sex, women cannot remove their egg from their body and place it in someone else's body. If sperm are nearby and the egg is fertile, the egg will activate and interact with the sperm, helping them penetrate the egg surface, but until then, the egg stays where it is and waits. It does not leave the body in search of a substance that can impregnate it.

Men *can* control when they ejaculate. Men can control how often they ejaculate. Men can actively choose to remove sperm from their own body and place it into someone else's body. And men's sperm are active. Upon ejaculation, sperm immediately seek out an egg to fertilize.

Ovulation and implantation are involuntary processes. Ovulation happens whether or not there is sex. Ovulation happens approximately monthly without resulting in pregnancy. Ovulation only leads to pregnancy when a man chooses to ejaculate and add his sperm.

Sperm fertilize. Eggs are fertilized.

Ovulation is involuntary. Ejaculation is voluntary.

BIRTH CONTROL FOR WOMEN IS HARD TO ACCESS AND HARD TO USE.

Female contraception is a modern miracle that has changed the lives of countless women for the better.

United Nations estimates from 2019 show that 842 million people worldwide use modern methods of contraception. (Modern methods include things like the Pill and other hormonal birth control options, IUDs, and sterilization procedures like tubal ligations.) In the United States, 90 percent of married women have used birth control. 93 percent of single women with long-term partners have used birth control. 99 percent of women who identify as religious—mainline Protestants, evangelical Protestants, and Catholics—have used birth control. 88 percent of all women have used contraception. Even 81 percent of US women who don't have insurance still manage to use birth control.

I don't think I personally know a woman who has never used birth control. That includes the women I know who are not sexually active and women who don't have or are not having sex with men, because birth control can be prescribed for many health reasons beyond preventing pregnancy. I'm grateful for birth control. I'm grateful that there are options. I'm grateful it works well for so many women. I'm grateful that I see very little stigma or shame around taking birth control. But we shouldn't forget that using birth control is a responsibility—and often a burden.

Hormonal birth control options for women—starting with the Pill—have been around for more than sixty years and are so commonplace that we talk about birth control like it's really simple to access and use. Just pick up a pack of Pills when you're grabbing a bottle of ibuprofen, easy peasy.

But that's not actually true. It's not true about the Pill, and it's not true about any forms of birth control for women.

Female contraception—Pill, Patch, Ring, Shot, IUD—requires a prescription. For women, this means that access to any form of common birth control starts with a doctor's appointment and a physical exam.

No big deal, right? It's just a doctor's appointment. All you have to do is find a heathcare provider who's taking new patients; have health insurance; double check that the doctor takes your insurance; wait six weeks for the next available appointment; come up with money for the co-pay; take off work, miss school, or find childcare to attend the appointment; and then lay on the exam table with your legs in stirrups while the doctor explores your most sensitive parts with cold metal medical tools. After that, you'll need to find a pharmacy and stand in line for forty-five minutes to fill your prescription. Or, if you're lucky enough to have a fixed address, you could set up an account with an online pharmacy and have the birth control delivered (be sure to monitor your account to make sure deliveries are happening on time and the prescription is up to date).

If the birth control the doctor prescribed isn't working for you, you'll need to make additional appointments to discuss other options or work out the kinks. And depending on what type of birth control method you decide on, there could be follow-up appointments—to have an IUD inserted or to get a quarterly shot. If a birth control method is working well for you, you still need to repeat this doctor appointment process at least once a year in order to keep the prescription current, and, if you're on the Pill, the

Patch, or the Ring, you'll need to monitor your online pharmacy account and update it with your new prescription or go to the pharmacy regularly to fill your prescription. Oh. Don't forget, if you move to a new city at any point, you'll have to begin the process all over again starting with a search for a new doctor.

If you're underage and want a birth control prescription, you'll likely have to involve your parents, which for some can be terrifying or impossible. If you're over eighteen and are trying to get birth control for the first time on your own, it can still be terrifying.

If you don't currently have a sexual partner, you may put off the doctor's appointment until further notice or let your prescription lapse. Then you have to start all over again if you ever become sexually active in the future.

To make matters more challenging for those hoping to avoid unwanted pregnancies, there are people actively working to make it even harder to access birth control. In July 2020, the Supreme Court ruled that private employers who hold religious or moral objections to birth control aren't required to include no-cost contraception options as part of their employee health insurance plan. Then, in June 2022, following the overturning of *Roe v. Wade*, Supreme Court Justice Clarence Thomas signaled that *Griswold v. Connecticut*, the case legalizing the use of contraception by married couples, could be up for reversal as well.

So yes, procuring and maintaining birth control for women is more complicated and challenging than we like to think it is. But once a woman successfully fills her prescription, happily it's smooth sailing.

Just kidding!

The list of side effects for the Pill/Patch/Ring/Shot is long and serious, including depression, fatigue, headache, insomnia, mood swings, nausea, breast pain, vomiting, weight gain, acne, bloating, blood clots, heart attack, high blood pressure, liver cancer, and stroke. Also, depending on where a woman is in her menstrual cycle, it can take two to seven days before the effectiveness even kicks in. So you can't fill a prescription and be instantly protected.

For copper IUDs, some women report significant daily bleeding for months or more than a year. This means pads, tampons, or managing a menstrual cup *every single day* for an undetermined amount of time, plus the accompanying laundry and changes of bedding. All of that takes time, energy, and resources, and it adds up quickly. For hormonal IUDs, menstrual bleeding can become unpredictable—for some it's reduced to almost nothing, for others it means longer periods but with less bleeding. Other IUD side effects can include: headaches, acne, breast tenderness, mood changes, pelvic pain, and increased menstrual cramps. If you're considering an IUD, have fun making the exciting choice between an IUD with hormones and their side effects and an IUD that brings on super heavy, intense periods.

You also have to pay attention, because there are medicines that impact the efficacy of hormonal birth control, like certain antibiotics, antifungals, and antinausea drugs.

Not all women experience the side effects, and not all women are bothered by the side effects they do experience. But for many, the side effects of birth control are a deal-breaker. And they should be.

Most women aren't actually told much about the risks of birth control, and if they do experience side effects, they are just expected to live with them. *No complaints, please. That's just how birth control is. Millions of women take this, so whatever you're dealing with can't be that bad. If you want to be sexually active, this is the price you have to pay. Suck it up.*

Consider the Johnson & Johnson COVID-19 vaccine, which was paused for ten days when a risk of blood clots was discovered. Six people out of the seven million who had received the Johnson & Johnson vaccine developed serious blood clots. One of them died. At the time, it was scary to read the headlines, though the risk of blood clot from the Johnson & Johnson vaccine is less than one in a million.

In contrast, the common forms of women's birth control come with a much higher risk of blood clots—oral contraceptives triple the risk of blood clots. According to the FDA, the risk of birth control users developing a serious blood clot is three to nine out of 10,000 each year (and 327 million people are taking hormonal birth control worldwide).

Based on what we know right now, birth control is riskier than any of the COVID-19 vaccines. And yet, it is prescribed daily without hesitation, often beginning at age thirteen or fourteen (sometimes younger).

Another point: Many women's birth control options require a woman to absorb hormones and/or suffer side effects, even on days when she is not having sex.

So let's picture how this works out in real life. Example one: A woman is married and on the Pill. Her husband is working out of town for the next three months, but he may be able to come home on some weekends. The woman takes the Pill—ingests hormones and deals with the side effects—every single day for those three months, even though she and her husband can rarely, if ever, have sex.

Example two: A single woman is dating and uses the Pill for pregnancy prevention. After a breakup, she has to decide: Should she keep taking the Pill? What if she finds her dream guy right away? What if she wants to be able to be sexually spontaneous? She decides to keep taking the Pill—ingesting hormones daily and dealing with the side effects—just in case, but she doesn't end up having sex with anyone for several months.

Men, consider what your girlfriend/wife/partner is doing for you. She's fertile 3 percent of the time and addressing her fertility 100 percent of the time, whether she has sex or not.

The good news is: birth control is so essential for most women that they make that doctor's appointment happily. As proof that women are steadfastly determined to be responsible about birth control, despite expense, inconvenience, daily hassle, maintenance, and side effects, consider that a whopping 90 percent of the $8 billion birth control market is made up of birth control options purchased by women.

Note No. 1

In conversations about the Pill, I've learned that a disturbingly high number of people are working under the assumption that a woman only takes the Pill right before she has sex, and that if she doesn't have sex that day, then she doesn't need to take the Pill. They're picturing it like an aspirin or ibuprofen for a headache—you only take it when you actually have a headache. But that's not how the Pill works. You have to take it every day no matter what, or it doesn't work, and you may need to take it for a full week after starting it before it is effective.

Note No. 2

You may be surprised to learn that the way women take the Pill is unnecessarily complicated. In a piece for The Conversation called "The way you take the contraceptive pill has more to do with the Pope than your health," Susan Walker details some of the history of the Pill, including how birth control pills simulate a menstruation schedule.

How so? Standard birth control pills are taken for twenty-one days, followed by a seven-day break, during which the woman takes a sugar pill or placebo (seven of the placebo pills come in the standard Pill pack of twenty-eight) and experiences vaginal bleeding. So women who take the pill have what seems like a "period" each month. But this "period" is manufactured and isn't even a little bit necessary. When a person stops taking the Pill for a week and takes the placebo instead, hormone levels drop, which causes the lining of the uterus to shed. But it's not the same as menstrual bleeding—the body isn't flushing out an egg—and technically, this "period" is called withdrawal bleeding.

Apparently, the seven-day break and its fake "period" was designed into the Pill as an "attempt to persuade the Pope to accept the new form of contraception as an extension of the natural menstrual cycle."

This attempt did not succeed, and the current Pope continues to forbid contraception in most cases. But the seven-day "break" is still a part of the Pill, and this unnecessary complication increases the chances for mistakes—mistakes that increase the risk of unwanted pregnancy. A great reminder that most everything about birth control is overly complicated and difficult, and men in power are largely responsible for these complications.

BIRTH CONTROL FOR MEN IS EASY TO ACCESS AND EASY TO USE.

Men have two options for birth control: condoms and vasectomies.

Both are easier, cheaper, more convenient, and safer than birth control options for women.

Condoms are sold in every grocery store, every pharmacy, every bodega, every gas station, every 7-Eleven. There are condom vending machines at nightclubs and in public bathrooms. They are available to purchase 24 hours a day, 365 days a year. They might be the most easily accessible product in the whole country.

Condoms are affordable. In the US, the average price for a box of thirty condoms is $10. And in all fifty states you can even access condoms for free. You can order them online and have them delivered to your home, or you can pick them up (no prescription needed, no permission needed, no questions asked) from clinics and other health organizations. Stop by the campus health clinic at your local college, and you'll often find a bowl of complimentary condoms for the taking.

Condoms are convenient. They don't require a doctor's appointment or an invasive physical exam of your most sensitive body parts, they don't require a prescription, and they are easy to find. They can be bought ahead of time and stored for three to five years. So you can purchase a box of condoms and be prepared without having to think—or do—much about it.

Condoms come in lots of varieties. There are different sizes, different materials, different lubrication options, even different flavors. If men find that they don't like the experience of sex with a certain brand of condom, they can try others until they find a favorite. If the man or his partner has an allergy to latex, they can opt for another material. And troubleshooting condoms doesn't require multiple doctor appointments.

Condoms make cleanup super easy. Condoms keep all the semen in one convenient little sack, which means semen won't get on bedding or clothing and won't drip from the woman's body as she waddles to the bathroom (bonus!).

Condoms are only used as needed. Men can use a condom when they are about to penetrate their partner—and not a second before. If they don't have sex that day, no condom needed. If they think they might have sex that day, but it turns out they don't, no condom needed. If they are away from their partner and can't have sex, no condom needed.

And finally, condoms work. When used correctly, condoms are 98 percent effective at preventing pregnancy. And not just that, condoms have double superpowers—they can prevent pregnancy, and they can prevent sexually transmitted infections (STIs). Women's birth control options do not have that same STI-fighting superpower.

What condoms don't have is a list of side effects. They don't cause depression, mood swings, blood clots, liver failure, weight gain, acne, strokes, or anything else on the list of side effects for hormonal birth control.

A highly effective birth control that is safe, affordable, and easily accessible? That you can stock up on? That only needs to be used for a short time during sex and has zero side effects? Five stars for condoms!

Not a fan of condoms? Men also have the option of getting a vasectomy. Vasectomies are safe, effective, and highly reversible. A vasectomy is a quick outpatient procedure with local anesthetic that takes place at a doctor's office and doesn't require a hospital stay.

Recovery from a vasectomy is easy, and most men return to work two to three days later and can resume physical activity in three to seven days. Recovery essentially looks like sitting in front of the TV with a bag of frozen peas. (I don't want to downplay soreness and pain, but if it makes you hesitant, I would like to take a moment to remind you that female contraception options, used by millions of women in our country and across the world, have well-known side effects that can be brutal and severe—and yes, also include soreness.)

Again, vasectomies are very safe, often covered by insurance, and the most reliable birth control option for men available at 99.99 percent effective. In other good news: Doctors are clear that after a vasectomy you will not experience any differences in your sexual function or pleasure. You will still be able to get an erection and ejaculate, and everything will feel the same.

Something to note: After your vasectomy, there can still be a few sperm in your system that will get flushed out with future ejaculations. You can have your doctor test a sample of your semen after twelve weeks or twenty ejaculations to make sure it's free of sperm. Until then, plan on using a back-up form of birth control. Those condoms in your drawer will work just fine.

As mentioned, vasectomies are highly reversible. Successful reversal rates are known to hover around 75 percent for vasectomies reversed within three years, with less success as the time between vasectomy and reversal attempt increased, but happily, things are improving. The Stanford Medical Center reports that, depending on the type of technique used, their vasectomy reversal success rate is 95 percent and makes clear that the length of time between the vasectomy and the reversal doesn't affect that success. The International Center for Vasectomy Reversal in Arizona, says, "Our experts can achieve a proven, published success as high as 99.5%." As far as vasectomy reversals go, we're clearly on a positive trajectory.

Be aware that despite these improvements in reversals, doctors still caution men against getting a vasectomy that they know they will want to reverse—after all, the patient may not be able to find a doctor skilled in the procedure, and reversal procedures are currently quite expensive. But we can be hopeful this may change as successful reversal numbers continue to get better and better.

Further improving vasectomy and reversal techniques would mean men could get a vasectomy when they are ready to be sexually active and then reliably reverse it if they and their partner want to conceive. This already happens sometimes; it's not uncommon for a man to get a vasectomy after he thinks he's done having children, only to reverse it when he and a new partner want to have a child.

Working toward making vasectomies and reversals a common and reliable birth control option for every man is a worthwhile goal. Of course, if reversal success is a worry, men can always bank their sperm before the vasectomy.

Birth control options for men are very effective plus vastly easier, safer, more convenient, more accessible, and more affordable than birth control options for women. Given this, the expectation ought to be that a man uses a condom every time he has sex. And if a man is deeply condom-averse, it should be an absolute given that he would get a vasectomy.

Note No. 1

Men also have a bonus "built-in" birth control. It's called the Pull-Out Method. You may want to yell at me and tell me it's irresponsible to even suggest pulling out as a birth control method, and I totally get where you are coming from. But I suggest the effectiveness is still much better than nothing. The Planned Parenthood website section on the Pull-Out Method says:

For every 100 people who use the pull-out method perfectly, 4 will get pregnant. But pulling out can be difficult to do perfectly. So in real life, about 22 out of 100 people who use withdrawal get pregnant every year—that's about 1 in 5.

So, the Pull-Out Method is 96 percent effective when men do it perfectly. I realize that 96 percent is not as good as the effectiveness of the Pill (99 percent) or condoms (98 percent) or a vasectomy (99.99 percent), but it's still pretty darn effective.

But as Planned Parenthood confirmed, pulling out can be difficult to do perfectly, so the Pull-Out Method is actually only 78 percent effective. That's not nearly as comforting as 96 percent, but it's still way, way better than doing nothing at all.

When learning that 78 percent statistic, a responsible man would not respond: *Well, the Pull-Out Method isn't effective enough, so I won't bother.* But rather: *I'd better learn what mistakes to avoid with the Pull-Out Method. This is serious business. I can't mess around with someone else's life like that. Part of my becoming an adult means I need to know how to pull out effectively and to do everything I can, like using condoms or considering a vasectomy, to make sure it doesn't come to that in the first place.*

Is this asking too much? We expect women to use their birth control perfectly, to remember to take the Pill daily, to keep up with doctor's appointments and prescriptions. Why shouldn't we expect men to use their birth control methods perfectly as well?

Note No. 2

Yes, internal condoms, or condoms for women, exist, but they are less effective, more expensive, and harder to find than male condoms, and in some areas, they require a prescription. They can be noisy, and they only come in one size. For these reasons, they are not a popular option for pregnancy prevention. Condoms for men are by far the easiest, safest, cheapest form of birth control.

Note No. 3

Important: When condoms are not used correctly, they are not as effective. That brings up the question: Is it fair to expect men to use condoms correctly? The answer is a strong yes. If women are expected to learn how to use their complicated birth control correctly, we can expect the same thing from men regarding their much-easier-to-use option.

To learn how to put on and remove a condom correctly, a man needs to practice. Practice is necessary to find his correct fit and material preference. Practice is also needed to figure out lubrication techniques (for example, adding a few drops of lubrication inside the condom). Successful condom users report that once they solved the size, materials, and lubrication questions, they could barely tell a difference between sex with a condom and sex without.

Again: If women are expected to learn how to use their birth control correctly, the same can be expected of men.

SOCIETY CLINGS TO THE IDEA THAT MEN HATE CONDOMS.

Condoms are simple, easy, and convenient, so why don't men use them every time they have sex? Anytime I've posed this question to an audience, the answer is swift and consistent: Men hate condoms.

I don't think anyone would argue with the premise that there is a pervasive perception in American culture that men prefer condom-less sex. Why this preference? Because we've been told (in books, in movies, in memes) that it doesn't feel as good as sex without a condom. (Meaning it doesn't feel as good *for men*. What it feels like for their partner doesn't really enter into the discussion.)

If men assume that sex with a condom doesn't feel as good as sex without a condom, then it it's easy to imagine that a man might wear one only if a woman insists, and only if he can't talk her out of it. Every few months, I see another viral tweet/TikTok from a woman talking about how often men try to convince women to have sex without a condom. These posts always have tens or even hundreds of thousands of likes and hearts and comments. Why? Because so many people find them relatable.

On June 25, 2022, a designer who goes by @studio lemaine tweeted: "It is very difficult and emotional to read 'no one is forcing you to have unprotected sex' when men do. All the time. Boyfriends and partners and abusers—the whole spectrum. Men pressure us for unprotected sex all the time."

The stereotype of men trying to avoid using condoms is basically a given in our culture. (The "why" behind the stereotype sometimes feels innocent, but other times it can be upsetting—some men describe feeling like it's a conquest to convince a women not to use a condom, and conversely, some men describe feeling less manly if they can't convince a woman to let them forego the condom.)

But what if our cultural myths around condoms are wrong? I don't have a penis and have never worn a condom, so I'm going to rely on the words of a man I spoke to when writing this book:

> *There is some truth to the idea of sex with a condom being less fun, but it's because condoms require practice. Men who have practiced using condoms and experimented with different varieties and use lubrication know that condoms don't diminish their pleasure during sex in any significant way.*

That's just one man, but I've also heard variations on this from hundreds of men whenever I host conversations online about this topic. So could it be that the accepted idea that condoms make sex less pleasurable—an idea that does a lot of harm to a lot of people—is wrong? Perhaps the problem isn't condoms but the way we talk about condoms. Or, more accurately the way we *don't* talk about condoms—if a man believes sex without condoms is a conquest, he's not likely to talk about the benefits of condoms with other men he knows.

Because of the cultural myths around condoms, and because it's considered a private topic, even men who don't have issues with condoms and don't find them less manly may not share their condom knowledge and experience. If a man finds the perfect condom or the perfect lubrication technique, he might keep this information to himself—which is a bummer, because studies have shown that when friends and confidants discuss condoms, it increases condom use. A man could have no issues with using condoms, but it's very possible that the men he interacts with won't know this. And so the assumption that men in general hate using condoms persists.

Related myths about loss of manliness hover around the topic of vasectomies, too. Many men worry that a vasectomy will risk messing up their erections or ejaculations. Men are concerned that they won't be able to "perform" after a vasectomy, that they'll be less virile. Because of this, in the United States, only 9 percent of men who are sexually active get vasectomies (but 27 percent of women who are sexually active get tubal ligations).

Again, because of privacy issues and the stigma around vasectomies, men don't often talk to other men about their experiences or the advantages. But the advantages are real. The cost savings and time savings of a vasectomy, year after year, are significant. But the biggest advantage may be psychological. Couples commonly report much improved sex lives after a vasectomy. Why? Because unwanted pregnancy stress is eliminated. Disappeared! Men also frequently report that the procedure is quick and easy, almost pain-free, and the recovery is straightforward and simple.

VASECTOMIES ARE LESS RISKY THAN TUBAL LIGATIONS.

Tubal ligations, aka tubals, aka "getting your tubes tied"—where the woman's fallopian tubes are tied off, cut, clamped, banded, sealed off with an electric current, or blocked—are often compared to men's vasectomies. This is understandable, because they are both considered permanent forms of birth control. But in practice and lived experience, vasectomies are easier and less risky.

A tubal ligation is a minor surgery—usually only thirty minutes—which involves one to two cuts through the abdomen. It requires either general anesthesia or spinal anesthesia (a type of local anesthesia that leaves you awake) and is performed at a hospital or outpatient surgical clinic. Most patients are able to go home the day of surgery but are instructed to wait several hours after the surgery before they leave the hospital or surgical clinic; they are further instructed that they should not drive themselves home or do any heavy lifting for approximately three weeks.

Vasectomies are outpatient procedures—usually only fifteen minutes—that happen in a doctor's office with a local anesthetic, and the patient can drive himself home immediately afterward.

Doctors and healthcare providers agree tubals are more invasive, riskier, and more complicated than vasectomies.

WebMD says: "If you're in a committed relationship, your husband or partner might be willing to get this procedure that keeps sperm from getting into his semen. It's a safer procedure than a tubal ligation, and it can be done while he's awake."

Spermcheck Vasectomy Research Center says:

When you look at the pros and cons, the scales tip in favor of vasectomies. Despite the facts, tubal ligation is still the more popular method. Maybe it's because birth control and sterilization are considered the woman's responsibility. But as many women will argue, and several guys have agreed with, women's bodies have gone through plenty of trauma with childbirth, so when it comes to sterilization, it's time for guys to take one for the team.

Dr. Alexander Pastuszak of the University of Utah Medical Center says:

With tubal ligation you need to make an actual hole in the abdomen, which by surgical standards is a minor surgery, but it's still much more major than a vasectomy. I don't see any reason why a tubal ligation would be or should be preferred over a vasectomy.

In a conversation on Twitter, a doctor said to me:

I do anesthesia for a living, done it for hundreds of tubals I'm sure. I often think: WTF is wrong with the husband? Except when part of a C-section, tubals should be rare. Vasectomies are cheap, low-pain, extremely safe, and highly effective. Why are tubals also a burden that women must carry? An additional point: there has never been a documented death from a vasectomy. However, many women have died from anesthetic or surgical complications from a tubal ligation.

It's not just that it's riskier than a vasectomy. Tubal ligations are routinely denied to women who are under thirty-five or who don't have kids. And not for the reasons outlined above, but because we have a paternalistic medical system that believes women aren't capable of making decisions about their own bodies. In fact, though it's not a legal requirement, it's also not uncommon for a doctor to require a woman to get the signature of her husband before they are willing to perform a tubal ligation.

Other factors:

- Though both tubals and vasectomies can be reversed, vasectomy reversals have a higher reversal success rate.

- Vasectomy reversals are a minimally invasive procedure, while tubal ligation reversals are described as major surgery.

- Women experience an increased risk of a tubal (ectopic) pregnancy if pregnancy occurs after a tubal ligation. Please note: an ectopic pregnancy requires immediate medical treatment.

- The side effects of a tubal ligation include perforation of the intestine, damage to the bowels, infection, and prolonged pelvic or abdominal pain. The side-effects for vasectomy are less severe and include swelling, bruising, and pain.

- After tubal ligation, some women report experiencing a rapid decline in the hormones estrogen and progesterone. It's called post–tubal ligation syndrome (PTLS), and has symptoms similar to menopause—like hot flashes, night sweats, trouble sleeping, a lower sex drive, and irregular periods. (The existence of PTLS remains controversial among doctors, but we should keep in mind how often women are disbelieved in medical contexts.)

- Vasectomy procedures have a lower cost than tubal ligations. In my research, I saw price ranges for vasectomy from $300 to $1,000 and tubal ligation price ranges from $1,500 to $6,000.

It should be very clear that when a couple is deciding between a vasectomy for the man or a tubal ligation for the woman, the vasectomy should be the easy choice every time.

WE EXPECT WOMEN TO DO THE WORK OF PREGNANCY PREVENTION.

The reigning assumption is that if a woman doesn't want to be pregnant, then she'll do whatever it takes to prevent a pregnancy from happening. After all, it's women's bodies that are stuck dealing with the pregnancy.

This assumption seems to align with data from the birth control industry. In 2019, The US contraceptive market size was valued at around $8 billion. Of the dozens of contraceptive products, approximately 90 percent of them are created for women, purchased by women, and used by women. That includes women purchasing more than 30 percent of male condoms.

Women who are sexually active are expected to use birth control or an IUD. Women are also expected to insist that men use a condom, which implies that women should keep condoms stocked. (It creates one of those fun double binds women get to deal with—if she has condoms, she's a slut, but if she doesn't have condoms, she's irresponsible.)

We don't even notice that women pay the costs of birth control, even though it benefits both men and women. In fact, I've never met a woman who charges her boyfriend for half the costs of the doctor's appointments, transportation, and prescription refills required of her to handle pregnancy prevention.

To be clear, men may not expect their girlfriend to help with the costs of condoms either, but the differences in cost between condoms and birth control (dollars, time, convenience, forethought, etc.) are significant, pennies to dollars. And as already mentioned, women also purchase more than 30 percent of condoms.

You might think women would be angry at men about all this. But mostly, we're not. We've been raised in the same culture as men. We've been taught the pleasure and convenience of men are paramount. We've been taught to diminish our own pain. And the lessons have stuck. We've taught those same lessons to others.

Even though birth control options for men have a long list of distinct advantages, we've put the burden of pregnancy prevention on women. We've put the burden on the person who is fertile for 24 hours a month, instead of the person who is fertile 24 hours a day, every day of their life.

WE DON'T MIND IF WOMEN SUFFER, AS LONG AS IT MAKES THINGS EASIER FOR MEN.

In 2016, the World Health Organization conducted a trial for male birth control—a hormonal injection that would lower sperm count. The results were very promising, showing a 96 percent effectiveness rate at preventing pregnancy. But even with the positive results, the trial was stopped. A committee determined the side effects of the drug were risking the safety of the study participants.

The most common side effects were acne and weight gain, which are also very common side effects for women's birth control. The most serious side effects for the men was that one participant became depressed and another suicidal. Which I agree is very serious. But side effects for women's birth control options are just as serious, if not more so—yet millions of women are still prescribed these drugs and ingest them daily.

That story perfectly captures an unspoken cultural maxim: *We don't mind if women suffer, as long as it makes things easier for men.*

Another medical example is "The Husband Stitch." Some doctors put in an extra stitch when repairing episiotomies or tearing from childbirth. The idea is that the stitch will tighten the vagina and provide increased pleasure for a male sexual partner. Unfortunately, the extra stitch can create painful consequences for women, including excruciating pain during sex.

Some women don't find out they've been given a husband stitch until they have a gynecological appointment with a new provider, a postpartum checkup, or a subsequent pregnancy. They might go in for a pap smear and the doctor sees the childbirth repair was made too tightly.

List of side effects for the male birth control trial:	List of side effects for women's hormonal birth control:
Acne	Acne
Headaches	Headaches
Mood swings	Mood swings
Tiredness/Fatigue	Tiredness/Fatigue
Weight gain	Weight gain
Depression	Depression
Mild erectile dysfunction	Bleeding or spotting between periods
Reduced sex drive	Bloating
	Feeling dizzy
	Fluid retention
	Increased appetite
	Insomnia
	Melasma (dark patches on the face)
	Nausea
	Tenderness or pain in the breasts
	Vomiting
	Blood clots
	Gallbladder disease
	Heart attack
	High blood pressure
	Liver cancer
	Stroke

Some men don't know a Husband Stitch has been made either, because the doctor just decided to do one on their own. And some men know about the stitch and don't like it—because it causes pain for themselves, or because it causes pain for their wife.

The thing is, the Husband Stitch *doesn't actually make a vagina tighter*. The man who requests the stitch or is happy about the stitch may get satisfaction from the idea that his partner's vagina is "tighter," but he won't actually feel a difference. His psychological satisfaction is prioritized over the women's physical pain.

And then there is IUD insertion. In discussions about pain management for men versus women, I see the example of vasectomies and IUDs brought up quite a bit. I've heard a vasectomy is about as invasive and painful as getting an IUD implanted. I've also heard IUD insertion is much more painful than a vasectomy. I've heard of women who didn't feel much pain at all while getting an IUD and other women who almost passed out from the pain. And I've heard from men who said they went straight from the vasectomy to a ballgame and didn't miss a beat. (I have yet to encounter a man who experienced a vasectomy as excruciating, but I can imagine one is out there.)

Those are all valid experiences and observations. I honor and believe each one. But here's the thing, vasectomies are *always* performed with at least a local anesthetic, while pain meds are *rarely if ever* used for IUD insertions. Let me say that again: these two procedures—one for men, and one for women—are both invasive and both involve very sensitive body parts. It's expected that the procedure will be painful for men, so pain relief is always administered. For women, it's expected that if it is painful, the women will just endure it, and pain relief is almost never administered.

I was especially interested to learn that the administration of general anesthesia (which is a serious procedure in its own right) is the only thing that has been shown to consistently remove the pain of IUD insertion. Should women be allowed to choose between the risks of general anesthesia and the risk of pain during an unmedicated IUD insertion? Or should the medical field just keep choosing for women, by not offering pain medication at all and telling women "it will just be a pinch."

Casey Johnston wrote an excellent essay that explores this contradiction, called "If Men Had to Get IUDs They'd Get Epidurals and a Hospital Stay." An excerpt from the essay:

A surprising number of people, as I discovered while trying to determine if my own acute suffering post IUD-insertion was abnormal, describe it as the worst pain they've experienced in their life. The worst of it is blinding and minutes long, and then about 75 percent of that pain goes on for hours. And that's if nothing goes wrong, like the device jams, and the doctor has to try again a second time.

To give a sense of the pain, or at least how bad the pain can be, if a shot is a 3 on a pain scale, an IUD insertion is a 10, in three waves. For an IUD insertion, on average, women receive virtually zero pain management before, during, or after: maybe a little numbing gel, maybe a single over-the-counter-strength painkiller afterward, and that's it.

The lack of pain relief offered is inhumane, but also an everyday occurrence.

One more example: In the early 1990s, researchers were studying a drug called sildenafil citrate. The hope was that the drug would help prevent and/or solve heart conditions. As the study progressed, the drug showed promising results for another condition: a fix for "penile winter," more commonly known as erectile dysfunction. The panel of decision-makers who were funding the study decided they would pursue the research for erectile dysfunction. Eventually the drug came to market. It was called Viagra.

In subsequent tests for the same drug, sildenafil citrate, they discovered that it also offered significant and lasting relief for women suffering from serious period pain.

That same team of decision-makers, all of whom were men, decided against pursuing research on menstrual cramp relief. Why? They believed that cramps were *not a public health priority*.

Not a public health priority? Research says that 80 percent of women experience menstrual cramps and/or period pain. Since at least half of the entire population of Earth experiences menstruation, that means there are approximately 3.1 billion people who have had to deal with period pain. To me, that certainly seems like a significant enough number to justify continued research.

Just imagine that. You're on a drug-testing committee, and you need to make a choice. On the one hand, you can choose to make it easier for older men to achieve and maintain an erection. On the other hand, you can choose to relieve women's suffering from serious period pain. And you choose the erections. Why in the world would you not choose both? I know. I know. It's probably money. But even that isn't adding up for me. 64 million men worldwide have been prescribed Viagra since 1998. That's a lot of people. But the potential market for period pain is 3.1 *billion* people.)

This little snippet of medical history is a variation on the maxim I mentioned above: When the choice is between maximizing men's pleasure or minimizing women's pain, society will predictably choose men.

When it comes to birth control, and really, life in general, we favor preserving men's convenience, peace of mind, and pleasure over preventing or relieving women's suffering.

Note No. 1

I'm not sure how to explain just how much women are accustomed to dealing with pain. Pain for women is normalized. Just gave birth? *Take an ibuprofen.* Getting an IUD? *It'll take too long to wait for an anesthetic, it's just a little pinch, just breathe through it.* It's both misogynistic and bizarre that it is considered completely normal to perform invasive gynecological procedures with no pain management.

SOCIETY TEACHES THAT THE MAN'S PLEASURE IS THE PURPOSE AND PRIORITY OF SEX.

A typical sex ed class in the United States will cover women's internal reproductive organs—ovaries, fallopian tubes, etc.—but doesn't explore the pleasure-related clitoris (how it works, how it's stimulated, how it connects to a female orgasm). Many don't even mention the clitoris. The same is not true for the pleasure-related penis.

To be clear, I'm not suggesting that sex ed classes are focused on male pleasure, I'm just pointing out that the penis definitely comes up in sex ed (pun intended). Erections are explained. Ejaculations are explained. The pleasure men experience during sex—arousal and orgasm—are just presented as part of the basic mechanics of sex.

It's taken for granted that men will experience pleasure during these sexual interactions. Will women experience pleasure in the same interactions? Who knows? It doesn't come up, because a woman's orgasm isn't an essential part of learning about the birds and the bees.

But it's not just sex ed classes. The way society talks about sex or presents sex is most often from a man's perspective. In fact, most studies of "how long intercourse lasts" are based on how long it takes for a man to ejaculate in a vagina.

According to conventional portrayals of the sex act, it's not over until the man ejaculates, and once he ejaculates, it's over. We're focused on the man's experience, not the woman's.

If a man has an orgasm and ejaculates in a vagina, most people would consider that to be sex. What if the woman doesn't orgasm in that same interaction? Is it still considered sex? Yes. Most people still call that sex. It's not the only way to define sex, but it's a common one.

I am going to speculate that our societal focus on the man's experience during sex feeds the resistance of some men to use condoms. Here's how I imagine the thinking goes: If sex is about the man's experience, then a man will prioritize his own pleasure and not suggest a condom. He won't bring condoms up at all (and hope that the woman he's having sex with won't either). This will all seem perfectly justifiable in his mind, because again, society has taught him (and all of us) that sex is about his experience, and his pleasure.

But what are we talking about pleasure-wise? How different is the pleasure of sex with a condom and without? Let's imagine a physical pleasure scale where 0 is neutral and 10 is maximum pleasure. A good massage lands at around 5 on the scale and an orgasm without a condom at 10. On this scale, where would sex *with* a condom fall? A 7? Maybe an 8? So, it's not that sex with a condom is *not pleasurable*, it's just not *as pleasurable*. An 8 instead of a 10.

Which brings us to a really disturbing conclusion. When men choose to have condom-less sex, they are putting a woman's body, health, social status, job, economic status, relationships, and even her life, at risk in order to experience a few minutes of *slightly* more pleasure. It's horrible to type it out. It gives me a stomachache just thinking about it. Would men really choose a few moments of slightly more pleasure over risking a woman's whole life?

Yes. Yes they would. It happens every day. It's as common as dandelions. We could say men are extremely inconsiderate, but I think it's more a matter of: 1) men not understanding or not appreciating what this actually means for women, 2) a culture that reinforces this ignorance, and 3) the all-too-human mandate to maximize pleasure, even at the disregard of possible consequences.

But here's the thing, with women's lives on the line, it really shouldn't take much persuasion to make men appreciate the consequences of unprotected sex and to push our culture to frown on this ignorance. Can't we persuade men that they can act responsibly without really having to sacrifice pleasure?

Let's try this analogy. Think of another great pleasure in life, let's say food. Think of your favorite meal, dessert, or drink. What if you found out that every time you indulged in that favorite food you risked causing great physical and mental pain for someone you know intimately? Not definitely—eating the food might not cause any pain at all—but there's a real risk that it might. You'd probably be sad, but you'd never indulge in that food again, right? Not worth the risk.

Then, what if you found out, there was a simple thing you could do before you ate that favorite food, and it would almost eliminate the risk of causing pain to someone else. But the simple thing would make the experience of eating the food slightly less pleasurable. To be clear, it would still be very pleasurable, but slightly less so. Maybe you have to eat the food—let's say it's a slice of pizza—with a knife and fork when you'd rather eat it with your hands.

Would you be willing to make that simple compromise to eliminate the risk of causing pain—possibly even death—to someone you know intimately, every single time you ate your favorite food?

Of course you would.

OF COURSE YOU WOULD.

Note No. 1

When discussing the 1 to 10 physical pleasure scale, a man volunteered to me: "Realistically I think we're actually talking 9.75/9.8/9.9 as far as sex with condoms go. Believe me, I know this because I'm a man and really the difference is barely noticeable. It's disingenuous for guys to claim it is."

Note No. 2

In contrast to our focus on men's pleasure, when thinking about sex there's often no thought to women's pleasure. Even though culturally (and sadly, sometimes by men specifically) women's pleasure may be ignored or neglected, women are very much able to experience pleasure during sex. When masturbating, 95 percent of women orgasm. In first-time hookups with other women, they orgasm 64 percent of the time. But in first-time hookups with men, they orgasm only 7 percent of the time. So we know that when we ignore the experience of women's pleasure during sex, the problem isn't women's ability to orgasm. It's our cultural approach toward heterosexual sex and our focus on men's pleasure over everything else.

WOMEN CAN BE IMPREGNATED WITHOUT EXPERIENCING PLEASURE.

For men, orgasm and ejaculation are known to be a pleasurable experience. Technically the two have separate functions (there are instances of ejaculation without orgasm, and orgasm without ejaculation), but since they almost always happen at the same time, we treat them as the same thing. We use the terms interchangeably; whether we say a man orgasmed or a man ejaculated, we mean the same thing.

Since a man's orgasm/ejaculation is the function that moves sperm from his body and places it elsewhere, and since an orgasm/ejaculation is a pleasurable experience, it is easy to make the argument that impregnating a woman is a pleasurable experience. For men.

In contrast, we know that it's very possible for a woman to be impregnated while experiencing zero pleasure. A man and woman can be having sex, and the woman may not be experiencing any enjoyment at all. She doesn't have an orgasm, and yet, she can still be impregnated by the man. She may even be totally passive during a consensual encounter—just lying still, no thrusting, no pleasure, no real participation—and the man can still impregnate her. In fact, it's totally possible for a man to impregnate a woman even while she's experiencing excruciating pain.

A woman's orgasm or a woman experiencing pleasure during sex has nothing to do with causing a pregnancy. As far as researchers know, women's orgasms exist for pleasure only. Some think a woman's orgasm can help push sperm toward the egg. It's certainly a theory, but it's a weak one, and it's been debunked. It would mean that the woman would need to orgasm simultaneously with the man, or after the man has orgasmed, and we know from both research and anecdotal evidence that that's not a particularly common occurrence. The science is also firmly established that eggs can easily be fertilized without any orgasm from the woman at all. So any theory painting the woman's orgasm as an essential part of biological procreation just doesn't hold up.

A woman experiencing pleasure and orgasm has never caused a pregnancy.

Of course, this flies in the face of people bent on "slut-shaming" women and blaming women's libidos and "slutty" behaviors for unwanted pregnancies. Let's address that view head on:

When I write that a woman experiencing pleasure and orgasm has never caused a pregnancy, what this means is a woman can be the sluttiest slut in the entire world—she could do nothing but have orgasms all day and all night during penetrative sex with multiple partners and no unwanted pregnancies will ever occur unless a man ejaculates irresponsibly in her body.

Why are we talking about unwanted pregnancies? Because 99 percent of abortions are the direct result of unwanted pregnancy. And we need to understand very clearly that women enjoying sex does not cause unwanted pregnancies and abortion. What causes unwanted pregnancies and abortion? *Men* enjoying sex and having irresponsible ejaculations.

Note No. 1

Some might argue that men can impregnate someone without feeling pleasure or having an orgasm, because pre-ejaculatory fluid, or precum exists. Precum is a bodily fluid that sometimes comes out of the penis during sex before ejaculation/orgasm, and sometimes there are sperm present in precum.

How often are sperm found in precum? Researchers don't really know. A 2016 study found 17 percent of the men in the study had sperm in their precum. But a 2021 study was inconclusive. We know that Planned Parenthood reports that the Pull-Out Method, when used perfectly, is 96 percent effective. Since pulling out perfectly or imperfectly wouldn't change the amount of sperm in precum, that 96 percent statistic suggests that sperm in precum is not especially common, or if they are common, it suggests that sperm found in precum aren't particularly effective at fertilization.

How do sperm end up in the precum in the first place? Again, the research isn't conclusive, but the most common theory is that earlier ejaculations can leave sperm in the pipes, and then the sperm leak out with the precum. If you're worried about sperm in precum, definitely use a condom. (And hey, condoms also protect both partners from STIs—using one is a good idea every time you have sex.) Convinced precum is a major cause of unwanted pregnancies? Well, I haven't found any data that backs that up.

Whether sperm is present from an at-the-moment ejaculation or sperm is present in precum from a previous ejaculation—the sperm are around because the man experienced an arousal and an orgasm/ejaculation. We can conclude that *a man can't impregnate a woman without feeling pleasure.*

MEN
CAUSE ALL
UNWANTED
PREGNANCIES.

If you're a man reading this book, the contrasts and imbalances between men and women that I've outlined so far may have come as a surprise to you, though they probably didn't make you defensive. But this section might. Because the argument I'm going to make is: All unwanted pregnancies are caused by irresponsible ejaculations. Or, in simpler terms: Men cause all unwanted pregnancies.

Yes, an egg is necessary in order for sperm to have something to fertilize, but there's a fundamental causal difference in the roles of the egg and sperm, and men have substantial control over where and when their sperm are released, while women have zero control over their eggs.

We've already established that women can't reliably and accurately predict when their egg is going to be fertile, but it's not just that. Eggs cannot be mobilized and directed to leave the body. During sex, a woman cannot keep her egg hidden away somewhere so that it's not exposed to sperm. Women cannot remove their egg before sex and set it aside and then put it back in their uterus when sex is finished. Yes, the egg moves to different positions within the reproductive system, but the woman can't control when those changes in position happen, and those changes in position are independent of a woman's sexual behavior. If a woman has sex, it doesn't mobilize or change the position of her egg. If a woman has an orgasm, it doesn't mobilize or change the position of her egg. If a woman *doesn't* have an orgasm, it still doesn't mobilize or change the position of her egg.

Unlike women and their eggs, men *can* mobilize and direct sperm to leave their body. That is what an ejaculation is. It's men choosing to direct sperm from their body and put it someplace else. During consensual sex, men get to choose if they will release sperm from their body, and men get to choose where they will put that sperm. They may put the sperm in a condom. They may have a vasectomy, in which case they keep their sperm to themselves and only ejaculate sperm-free semen. They might put the sperm on their partner's stomach. They might put the sperm in their hand. They might put the sperm in a tissue, a spare sock, a plant, or on a random spot on the floor or wall. Or they might put the sperm in a vagina and put their partner at severe risk for the complications of unwanted pregnancy.

You may be thinking: But if it's consensual sex, then they *both* caused the unwanted pregnancy!

65

Well, not really. Even in the case of consensual sex, the man gets final say. This is how it works:

Step 1: Woman consents to sex.

Step 2: Man decides if he will ejaculate responsibly.

A woman's consent to sex does not force a man to ejaculate in her vagina. Even if the woman says, "Pretty please have sex with me without a condom. I want you to ejaculate inside me," the words don't force the man to ejaculate inside her without a condom. He still has to choose. Ultimately only the man decides where his sperm ends up. Only he can choose what to do with his sperm and where it goes. A woman telling a man he doesn't have to wear a condom doesn't force that man to have sex with her without a condom. He has the right of refusal. If he chooses to have sex without a condom, then he is choosing to risk causing an unwanted pregnancy.

No matter what a woman "lets" a man do, she can't (legally) make a man ejaculate inside of her. When he does, that's 100 percent his doing. We know this is true because if she "let" him put his penis in a waffle iron, he wouldn't. If someone tells you to do an irresponsible thing, and you choose to do that irresponsible thing, that's on you.

To help us wrap our minds around this concept, let's consider two buddies making a video for TikTok. They have a gun, and Buddy #1 says, "Shoot me and let's film it." Buddy #2 says, "No way." Buddy #1 begs, "Come on man, it will be so cool, we'll go viral." Buddy #2 still refuses. He won't do it. Buddy #1 keeps pressuring, "Dude, just do it. If anything bad happens, it's on me; it's my idea." Buddy #2 is persuaded and decides to shoot Buddy #1. Buddy #2 pulls the trigger. His intention was just to wound Buddy #1, but his aim slips and the gunshot is fatal. Buddy #2 is convicted of manslaughter and goes to prison.

To be clear: Was Buddy #1 (the dead one) a fool? Was he acting irresponsibly? Yes. Yes to both of those questions. Buddy #1 definitely chose to act irresponsibly. He shouldn't have suggested the idea. He shouldn't have participated. But Buddy #1 making the suggestion *didn't actually kill anyone*. Standing in front of a gun may be stupid, but it is not a lethal action.

What about Buddy #2? Was Buddy #2 forced to pull the trigger? No. No he wasn't. It was ultimately his choice. Was Buddy #2 also acting irresponsibly? Yes, and his irresponsible actions got someone killed. All irresponsible actions in this scenario are not equal. Some actions are stupid, some are lethal.

Is it irresponsible if a woman agrees to have sex without a condom? Or if she suggests sex without a condom? Yes, it is. A woman suggesting sex without a condom is acting irresponsibly. I wish she wouldn't do that. And yet, her body can't cause a pregnancy. No matter how much sex she has, her orgasms cannot *cause* a pregnancy.

Yes, she chooses which man she says "yes" to. But her "yes" doesn't render him physically incapable of putting on a condom, saying "no," or getting a vasectomy. If a man chooses unprotected sex and puts his sperm in a woman's vagina, not only is he, too, being irresponsible, but in his case, his body *can* cause a pregnancy via his orgasm and sperm.

Again, all irresponsible actions in this scenario are not equal. Her actions—choosing to have sex and orgasm without a condom—are ill-advised. His actions—choosing to have sex and orgasm without a condom—can cause pregnancy.

I sense you still want to argue about this, so let's try another scenario. A woman and a man agree to have sex without a condom (conveniently for this scenario, he's among the majority of men who don't have sperm in their precum). He puts his penis in her vagina, starts his best moves, and shortly after, she has an orgasm, but he hasn't yet. As soon as her orgasm is finished, she stops and says "Thanks so much for the sex!" then gets dressed and leaves. Though they had sex, and though her egg was present, and though she had an orgasm, the women wasn't impregnated and could not be impregnated. The women successfully had unprotected sex with no risk of pregnancy because her male partner didn't ejaculate. Unprotected sex without sperm will not lead to pregnancy.

You might be thinking, well, that's not really sex, he didn't even ejaculate. But of course it's sex. When the opposite happens, when the man has an orgasm quickly, and then stops having sex before the woman has an orgasm, that is still considered sex (and is famously common). If the penis goes into the vagina, that's penetrative sex, whether or not either person has an orgasm.

Ultimately, it's men who produce sperm that can fertilize an egg and cause a pregnancy. Men can easily prevent unwanted pregnancies that lead to abortion by choosing to ejaculate responsibly.

WE EXPECT WOMEN TO BE RESPONSIBLE FOR THEIR OWN BODIES AND FOR MEN'S BODIES.

Whenever I discuss this topic, I get a variation on this response: "All women need to do is ask men to wear a condom and then refuse to have sex with him if he doesn't." Sounds so simple! Problem solved. Except it's not.

It's true that women can refuse sex without a condom. And we know plenty of women insist on condoms every single day, all over the world. But I would also say: Why would a woman ever need to ask a man to wear a condom? Why wouldn't it be the default that men should provide their own condom and put it on without a request? Who benefits if the man doesn't wear a condom?

If a woman doesn't make the request—let's pretend she's preoccupied and forgets to ask—does that mean the man is off the hook? She didn't bring it up so therefore he doesn't need to wear a condom? He doesn't need to be responsible for his own bodily fluids? Of course he does.

If Person One knows they have an STI and transmits it to their partner, Person Two, in many states that's a crime, and Person One can be prosecuted by the state. Additionally, Person Two can bring a civil suit against Person One. If your bodily fluids have the potential to harm your partner, it's your responsibility to ensure they don't.

If a man sees evidence of birth control in a woman's house (like the Pill) or asks her if she's on birth control, and she answers yes, does that qualify as a man being responsible? And does her positive response absolve him of any obligation to wear a condom? If yes, why?

Perhaps you are thinking responsibility is fifty-fifty. The woman just needs to insist that the man use a condom. But hold up a minute. If the woman has to insist a man use a condom, haven't you just described an irresponsible man? How is that fifty-fifty? You just put 100 percent of the responsibility on the woman by saying she needs to insist the man use a condom. You're asking the woman to be responsible for her actions and also for the man's actions. So how is the man acting responsible in this scenario if he only wears a condom if the woman insists? Answer: He's not. Men can use a condom, get a vasectomy, or decline to have unprotected sex. If he does these things, he won't cause a pregnancy. Relying on his sexual partner to use birth control is avoiding or relinquishing his responsibility.

Here's another example. Pretend you have a child who lives with an infection, and the infection can be spread to others by contact with your child's blood. Happily, it's a manageable infection and doesn't affect your child's quality of life, but still, you would no doubt teach your child that they need to be very careful with their blood. If they get cut on the playground, then they are at risk of infecting someone else—maybe their teacher or one of their friends. As a parent, you would drive home the point over and over again and make sure your child had whatever they needed to prevent spreading the infection to someone else. You would expect your child to take responsibility for their blood, especially as they got older and understood the consequences of their actions.

If you have a son, his sperm can "infect" any woman he has sex with. As parents, as a culture, we need to emphasize how carefully sperm needs to be handled. Pregnancy and childbirth are known to kill women. Pregnancy and childbirth are highly likely to leave permanent scars and cause future health problems, including possible future infertility. Unplanned pregnancy and childbirth can have a significant negative impact on the quality of life for the future child and their parents.

A man's sperm can cause a huge amount of damage.

It is astounding and disheartening to say it, but our current culture doesn't actually expect men to be responsible for preventing pregnancy. Our current culture doesn't even expect men to provide their own condoms.

If a man causes an unwanted pregnancy, the pregnant woman is often asked how it could have happened. Why didn't she force the man to wear a condom? Doesn't she keep condoms stocked at her home? Which, when you think about it, is an odd thing to expect women to keep stocked. It's like a person with a newborn baby visiting a house where no babies live and being surprised the house isn't stocked with diapers and wipes and nursing bottles.

The thing is, even though it shouldn't be necessary, women often *do* stock condoms. It's not at all unusual for a woman to keep condoms in her bedside table. She just picks up a typical box and hopes the condoms will work for whoever needs them.

We could say that *everyone* should keep condoms stocked, just in case. It's simply good manners. In the same way I hope that men keep menstruation products on hand in their home even if no one with a period lives there.

In my research for this book, I've heard from a lot of wives and girlfriends. Women who are with men they love and trust and are building a solid life with. But these women come with stories. One, a mother of three with an IUD, told me she has bled every day for a year, that she hates the side effects of the IUD and has tried everything else. She wonders: Why hasn't her husband suggested a vasectomy? Another woman explained that she wanted lots of kids *eventually*, but that her husband "didn't like using condoms," and they ended up with four kids in five years—much faster than she had wanted and much faster than her body could handle without serious long-term damage. Again, these are women in stable, loving marriages, with men who try to be good husbands and fathers.

These stories show something clearly: We, men and women, have a huge blind spot when it comes to men and birth control. Men assume women will do all the work of pregnancy prevention, that a woman will take responsibility for her own body and for the man's body, and women assume women will do it, too.

WE NEED TO SHIFT OUR FOCUS TO MEN.

Any man who has had a vasectomy and/or who uses condoms regularly and correctly and/or declines to have unprotected sex with a woman is taking responsibility for what he does with his penis and where he ejaculates. Any man who isn't doing these things isn't taking responsibility. When asked what men can do to prevent unwanted pregnancies, if a man answers, "Well, the woman just needs to . . ." that's a clear indication that he has no actual interest in preventing unwanted pregnancies. He wants to focus on women, but he needs to focus on men.

If a man can easily prevent unwanted pregnancies by controlling his own actions, but he's only interested in preventing unwanted pregnancies if women are controlling the actions, it seems like he's much more interested in controlling women than he is in reducing unwanted pregnancies.

I understand the tendency is to stay focused on women. I can hear the familiar refrain: *She should have kept her legs closed! If she chose to have sex, then she chose to get pregnant.*

Yes. We love blaming women for enjoying sex. How dare she want to have sex? But that's so backwards. A woman having an orgasm while a man penetrates her risks nothing and hurts no one. A man having an orgasm while he penetrates a woman risks everything—he risks her body, her health, her income, her relationships, her social status, even her life, and he also risks creating another human being.

Here's the thing, if you're someone who is interested in reducing abortions, as strange as it sounds, focusing on abortions is not the answer. Neither is focusing on women. Women are already doing the work of pregnancy prevention.

No. If you actually want to reduce abortions, you need to start much earlier. Instead of focusing on abortions, you need to focus on preventing unwanted pregnancies. And to do that, you need to focus on preventing irresponsible ejaculations.

If your focus is solely on abortion and whether it is a legal or moral right, you still won't reduce the number of unwanted pregnancies, and you won't reduce the number of irresponsible ejaculations. But! If you focus on dramatically reducing the number of irresponsible ejaculations, you will dramatically reduce the number of unwanted pregnancies, and you will dramatically reduce the number of abortions.

So we can see that this focus on men is a practical decision. This is a one-way street, and we've been driving the wrong way. We need to focus on men and stopping irresponsible ejaculations. Everything else—reducing unwanted pregnancies, reducing abortions—follows from this critical focus.

HOLDING MEN ACCOUNTABLE FOR THEIR ACTIONS DOES NOT MAKE WOMEN VICTIMS.

At this point you may be thinking: *Men cause all unwanted pregnancies? This can't be right. This seems too unequal; it feels wrong. This removes agency and responsibility from the woman. Are we supposed to think women are just helpless creatures with no decision-making power in all of this? Aren't we painting women as weak? Aren't we making them victims?*

No. I'm not taking responsibility away from women, I'm just reminding men of theirs. Holding men accountable for their actions does not make women victims. Asking men to take some responsibility is not the same as allowing women to take no responsibility.

Bringing up the topic of men or their responsibilities is not actually a comment on women at all.

Let me offer up another analogy. Imagine two teens, Jennifer and David, are assigned to work on a group project at school. Jennifer is doing almost all the work. So someone says to David, "Hey, did you notice Jennifer is doing almost all the work? You really need to step up." Does that mean Jennifer no longer needs to do her work? No. It means David needs to be responsible for his part of the work and actually do it.

To hold men responsible does not imply that women have no control of their sex lives, or that they are only passive victims. If I say, "irresponsible ejaculations cause unwanted pregnancies," is that the same as saying women can't choose when to have sex, why to have sex, how to have sex, or with whom to have sex? No.

If the underlying worry is still the unfairness of saying men cause all unwanted pregnancies, if you're worried that women don't have to be responsible, put your mind at ease. Remember, if the man ejaculates irresponsibly and causes an unwanted pregnancy, the woman has no choice but to deal with that pregnancy. How is a woman ever absolved of the outcome of an unwanted pregnancy? She isn't. She can't be. Whether she endures the full pregnancy, has a miscarriage, or gets an abortion, she has to deal with it one way or another. On the other hand, can you think of common examples where the man is absolved of the consequences of unwanted pregnancy? (I can!)

If you think I should be holding women more accountable for preventing pregnancy, then you're in luck: Women are already held accountable for preventing pregnancy. Women already do the vast majority of the work of pregnancy prevention. The burden of birth control, the effects of birth control, and the consequences of failed birth control are essentially entirely on women.

Interestingly, when I point out that women are currently expected to do the vast majority of pregnancy prevention, I don't think I've ever heard someone say, "This can't be right. This seems too unequal; it feels wrong." The imbalance only seems to strike people as out-of-whack if it's applied to men. Consider this for yourself. Surely, if you felt that my mere suggestion that men cause all unwanted pregnancies is unfair, wouldn't you feel the same discomfort at the very true reality that women do almost all the work of pregnancy prevention? Isn't that just as unfair?

Women should be responsible for their own bodies and bodily fluids. They currently take on that responsibility, and they should continue to do so. I'm simply pointing out that men need to be responsible for their own bodies and bodily fluids as well.

A woman is 100 percent responsible for her own body and her own bodily fluids. A man is 100 percent responsible for his own body and his own bodily fluids. Pointing out that men have bodily fluids that can cause pregnancy, and therefore men need to take responsibility for those bodily fluids, does not remove accountability for women or make women victims. It doesn't say anything about women at all.

THE UNEVEN POWER DYNAMIC BETWEEN MEN AND WOMEN IS REAL AND CAN TURN VIOLENT QUICKLY.

The United States is a patriarchal society geared toward men's pleasure. The cultural pressure for a woman to favor a man's pleasure over protecting her own body is massive and not very well understood or acknowledged by our culture as a whole. Saying a woman should just insist on a condom ignores the uneven power dynamic that exists between men and women, maybe especially when it comes to sex. It's similar to saying that women who are being sexually harassed by their supervisor at work "just need to speak up," as if that's a simple, easy way to resolve the issue. We know it's more complicated than that.

POP QUIZ FOR MEN

It's very easy to say women simply have to demand the man wear a condom, but here are some questions to help you imagine what that actually means. As you read the questions, imagine the power dynamics at play.

○ Before sex, have you ever avoided bringing up condoms or birth control and waited for your partner to say something?

○ Have you ever hinted to your partner, or outright told her, that sex feels better without a condom?

○ Have you ever assumed your partner will have condoms or will otherwise be taking care of birth control?

○ Have you ever thought: Well, if she gets pregnant, she can just get an abortion or go buy the morning after pill?

○ Have you ever bargained with your partner that you won't wear a condom, but you promise to pull out?

○ Have you ever promised to pull out and didn't? (Be aware, that's assault.)

○ Have you ever removed a condom during sex without telling your partner? (It's called stealthing, and, yes, it's also assault.)

○ Have you ever told your partner that condoms don't work for you, that they don't fit you, that they always break when you use them?

○ Have you ever sighed or rolled your eyes at the suggestion of using a condom?

○ Have you ever assumed you don't need a condom because your partner is on the Pill?

○ Have you ever assumed that if you don't want to use a condom, it's up to your partner to say no to sex?

○ Have you ever refused a condom, then blamed your partner for not walking away and thought of her as the irresponsible one?

○ Do you think people should cover their mouth and nose when they sneeze so they don't spray germs everywhere, but you don't think you need to worry about where your sperm ends up?

○ Have you ever hinted that if your partner denies your request for condom-less sex, you'll hurt your partner, or make things difficult, painful, or otherwise unpleasant for her? (This is sexual coercion. If you know anyone that has done this, they should be in prison.)

○ Are you aware of the cultural, psychological, and emotional pressure for women to be the one who is solely responsible for preventing unwanted pregnancies?

○ Are you aware of the pressure for women to agree to having sex with no condom in order to not disappoint men, to not displease men, and to not risk lessening the pleasure of men?

○ Have you ever made jokes or laughed at jokes about men promising to pull out, but then not doing it? (Hahaha assaulting her and impregnating her against her will is so funny.)

○ Have you avoided getting a vasectomy because you think it will hurt, or that sex will be less pleasurable after, or that you'll be less manly, even though you think women should be willing to get an IUD (which can be equally painful and invasive but is administered without pain relief)?

○ Have you ever agreed to sex without a condom, even though you knew your partner wasn't on birth control? Why? Even if she agreed, why would you risk her health and life like that? Did you consider what kind of cultural pressure she must feel to agree to something that is essentially self-harm?

○ Do you understand that you and only you are 100 percent responsible for your own bodily fluids?

The reality women face is that if they say no to sex, or no to unprotected sex, the man may respond with violence and anger. This may be a difficult thing to imagine if you don't regularly go to bed with people who weigh twice as much as you do and can easily break your neck.

In discussions about this power dynamic and unwanted pregnancy, it's especially irritating when I hear a man say, "Why doesn't she just make him wear a condom?" Why do I find that so irritating? Because: 1) Men willingly admit they're terrified of other men—they don't like to confront other men or publicly criticize them for fear of repercussions. If men feel fear about confronting or criticizing other men, why wouldn't women? 2) Men are aware that, speaking generally, they often have twice the physical strength of women. 3) It's not a secret that some men become violent when rejected. And yet, knowing those three things, many men somehow think it's a simple, easy ask for a woman to insist a man use a condom, or deny him sex if he won't use one. If men were put in the same position as women—making an uncomfortable request of someone who may have twice their strength and could turn violent—would they be willing to do so?

Women may be emotionally rejected, they could be verbally assaulted or kicked out of their home with nowhere else to go, they could be hit or choked or otherwise physically assaulted, they could be raped. This anger could come from a man they don't know very well, but it is much more likely to come from a boyfriend, husband, or other established relationship.

In North America, one in four women will be sexually assaulted in their lifetime. In one study, 30 to 35 percent of men admit they would rape if they thought they could get away with it legally. In a poll of 22,000 women in Britain, 51 percent responded that they had woken to a partner having sex with them or performing sex acts on them. For many young women, violence has even become an expected part of *consensual* sex—if women aren't willing to be choked or slapped or otherwise hurt, they are labeled "vanilla" and rejected.

And there are many women who have engaged in consensual yet *coerced* sex, including women who are in abusive marriages or relationships. (When you're looking at stats, remember that coerced sex doesn't get counted in the nonconsensual numbers.) If the woman is impregnated and delivers a child, it means she's now tied to her abuser by custody. It means the abused person now has a child that the abuser can also abuse.

Murder is the leading cause of death for pregnant women, often committed by the man who impregnated them. If that doesn't underscore the power dynamic in sexual relationships, I don't know what will.

When data about abuse is brought up, it's common to hear refrains of: *Why don't women just pick better men? Why are they having sex with abusers?*

I mean ... do you have a list? A list of all the men women should avoid? If you have some surefire way to distinguish the abusive men from the non-abusive men, we'd all like to hear it. The reality is, men are no better at identifying the abusive men in their lives than women are. Statistically, every man knows abusers in real life—there are abusers among his coworkers, his neighbors, his group of friends, and his church congregation. But men don't seem to know which of the other men they know are abusive. So why would women be able to know this?

Don't ask: *Why don't women pick better men?* Instead, ask: *Why are there so many abusive men?* And: *Why don't we teach men not to abuse?*

The uneven sexual power dynamic is something we are all steeped in. Farida D., an Arab gender researcher and poet, describes this well in her book *The 8th List of Shit That Made Me a Feminist*:

Patriarchy teaches us that sex, for women, is a giveaway, *while for men it is a* takeaway.

She saves *herself, gives* herself *to the right one, and then her virginity is* lost. *In this equation, there is nothing in sex that's for her to* take. *Whereas he* takes *and* scores *and there is nothing in sex for him to* give. *When her mind is programmed to* give, *she struggles to say "no." When his mind is programmed to* take, *he struggles to accept "no."*

A WOMAN CAN'T WALK OUT ON A PREGNANCY.

Once a man causes an unwanted pregnancy, the woman doesn't get to decide whether or not to deal with the pregnancy. Eventually, she has to make choices. Should she continue the pregnancy and deliver the baby? Will she be able to keep her job? Will her family reject her? How will she pay for medical costs? Does she have resources to raise the child? Can she have an abortion? Is it allowed in her state? How far along is she? Does she have the funds to travel to another state if needed? Is adoption something she would consider? If yes, will she keep contact with the child throughout their life via an open adoption? Will she change her mind about relinquishing as the pregnancy continues or after the birth?

The man can opt out of this enormous physical and psychological burden.

When pointing out that irresponsible ejaculations cause all unwanted pregnancies, some people seem to think that if they accept this premise, that acceptance will magically change who ends up bearing the physical consequences of pregnancy. It makes us feel good to think that men could share the responsibility of their ejaculation with women. But share how? Does he carry half the pregnancy? Does he experience half the labor and delivery? Does he breastfeed half the days?

Men carry, abort, suffer complications from, labor, deliver, and die from 0 percent of unwanted pregnancies. Men can and do walk out on pregnancies. Women cannot.

WE'RE NOT HONEST ABOUT PREGNANCY AND CHILD-BIRTH.

The negative realities of pregnancy and childbirth—physically, emotionally, financially, and socially—are not accurately represented in discussions about abortion.

Anyone experiencing pregnancy and childbirth should expect permanent, negative changes to their body, including scarring, pain, and loss of function. That may sound like an extreme thing to say, but I would argue that it only sounds extreme because our culture consistently downplays what women experience during pregnancy and childbirth. As an example of this, I've had six textbook "healthy" pregnancies. And if you had asked me after each one if I had experienced scarring, pain, or loss of function, I would have thought of all the women I know who had medically terrifying pregnancies/childbirth and quickly replied, "No, my pregnancies were very straightforward with no big medical issues." And while it's true that my pregnancies *were* very straightforward, if I think about it for more than a moment, I can identify scarring, pain, and loss of function that my body has definitely experienced from pregnancy and childbirth.

If you look at it closely, the process of pregnancy and childbirth is quite horrifying. Two things can be true at once: Pregnancy and childbirth are mind-blowingly glorious and miraculous, AND they're some of the most dangerous and damaging things a body can experience.

Pregnancy and childbirth can change the skeletal structure of a body. The vagina can literally fall out after having a baby—it's called pelvic organ prolapse. It's common for feet to grow a full size or more (say goodbye to every pair of shoes you own). The mother can experience serious bone loss as the fetus absorbs calcium from the mother's body.

There can be shorter-term issues like hair loss, a broken coccyx, kidney stones, extreme nausea and vomiting that damages the esophagus, cracked ribs, massive blood loss, hemorrhoids, and healing from a third-degree genital tear with more than thirty stitches. There can be lifelong issues like chronic high blood pressure that can lead to stroke and a damaged pelvic floor that causes urine leaks every time you sneeze. Pregnancy and childbirth can bring on new allergies, depression, uterine infections, the need for gallbladder removal, rheumatoid arthritis, and infertility.

Pregnancy and childbirth can change how your body moves—when I ask women to tell me about what pregnancy and childbirth did to their bodies, I consistently get descriptions like: *Pregnancy made it so I can't reach up high or do sit-ups* and *I can no longer lie flat on my back on the floor.* A pregnant body may experience symphysis pubis dysfunction (SPD), also called pelvic girdle pain (PGP). This is caused when the hormones that allow your pelvis to pull apart during birth are released too early, and it can make it very difficult to walk.

Pregnancy and childbirth can change the way a body looks—episiotomy scars, vaginal scars, C-section scars, peripherally inserted central catheter line scars, and widespread scarring on the midsection, thighs, bottom, and breasts from rapidly stretching skin. Diastasis (abdominal muscle separation) is common. So is weight gain. And don't forget about saggy breasts.

Women are generally just expected to deal with these issues and body changes without complaint—to cheerfully accept that these changes are a part of motherhood. Some of these issues become cultural jokes, like a woman saying no thanks to jumping on the trampoline because she'll pee her pants if she does. I'm trying to imagine how our culture would react if men with children peed themselves every time they jumped or sneezed. I don't think the medical community would be okay with that. I think the issue would be solved by now. Speaking of which, some of the issues brought on by pregnancy and childbirth *can* be solved or improved with medical intervention, but insurance may or may not cover the costs depending on whether or not the procedure is considered cosmetic.

And then there is the pain. Pregnancy and childbirth *hurt*. Backaches, headaches, pinched nerves, stretching skin, swollen breasts. Despite how uncomfortable it can be, pain relief isn't typically offered during pregnancy, for fear of harming the developing fetus.

During labor and delivery, an epidural or spinal may be offered, but they aren't always reliable and come with their own sets of negative side effects. During the labor and delivery of my fourth child, I was given a spinal. Spinals wear off after a certain amount of time depending on the dose, and mine wore off before delivery. I was able to experience a respite from labor pains for a couple of hours but felt the full painful wrath of the delivery as well as the full pain of the hours and hours of contractions before the spinal.

When you push a human out of your body and tear the muscles and skin in your genitals, the postpartum pain management begins and ends with popping an ibuprofen (but not too many, because you don't want to poison your breast milk).

A lot of people like to picture pregnancy as a risk-free adventure, but pregnancy and childbirth can kill you. It's true that in prior centuries, dying in childbirth was far more common, and thankfully we've made huge strides in making the experience safer. And yet, it's still inherently dangerous. A few stats to illustrate that reality:

- Going through pregnancy and childbirth in the United States is nearly 1.5 times as likely to kill you as traffic accidents (there are 17.4 deaths per 100,000 pregnancies each year, and 11.7 deaths per 100,000 people from driving each year).

- Worldwide, maternal death rates are falling. At the same time, in the United States, maternal mortality rates are rising—they have more than doubled over the last three decades. These deaths are disproportionately of Black women, making it significantly more dangerous for Black women to experience pregnancy and childbirth.

- Across the world, 800 people die *every day* from pregnancy and childbirth-related causes.

- In the United States, 700 to 900 women die from causes related to pregnancy and childbirth *each year*.

- For each woman who dies, up to 70 suffer hemorrhages, organ failure, or other significant complications. That's approximately 49,000 to 63,000 people each year.

- The United States, one of the richest countries in the world, is ranked #56 in maternal mortality—that's dead last among industrialized countries.

- The leading cause of death for pregnant women in the United States is homicide, usually at the hands of an intimate partner.

Giving birth is dangerous work. Arguably it's the *most* dangerous work. We tend to think that the most dangerous work is done by men in predominantly masculine professions, like firefighters and police officers.

But our assumptions are wrong. As mentioned in the list above, in the United States, the mortality rate for pregnancy is 17.4 per 100,000 people. The on-duty murder rate for police officers is 13.5 per 100,000 people. Which means a pregnant woman is more likely to die due to that pregnancy than a police officer is to be killed on the job.

And it's not just that pregnancy and childbirth are more dangerous than other work, it's that 86 percent of women do this dangerous work—and most do it more than once. The future of the human race depends on the assumption that the vast majority of women will be willing to do this incredibly hard and dangerous thing.

There is nothing similarly dangerous that we assume 86 percent of men will be willing to do. This fact should really make us rethink our societal perceptions of risk and danger. If asked to list the bravest among us who do dangerous work or risky activities, I would expect people to name first responders or firefighters, rock climbers or skydivers—I doubt anyone would mention pregnant women.

Men famously can't handle the pain when connected to a menstrual cramp simulator. Men wouldn't accept the side effects from a male birth control pill. Yet men expect women to experience pregnancies that routinely maim them and can even kill them. I think it's safe to say that if sex were as risky for men as it is for women—with an unwanted pregnancy potentially leading to loss of social status, loss of career, a disruption of their education, physical disability, death, and the permanent responsibility for another human—that men would insist on having a choice in the matter.

Pregnancy is risky and dangerous. We can't have a meaningful discussion of unwanted pregnancy, or abortion, without acknowledging this fact.

So why don't we talk about the dangers of pregnancy and childbirth openly? Why aren't the risks common knowledge? I can think of two reasons:

First, there's a worry that if women acknowledge that their pregnancy and childbirth were difficult, it somehow implies that they didn't want their baby or don't love their child. Some women have a relatively easy time being pregnant, others don't. Regardless of their experience, most women are pressured to say they are enjoying the pregnancy.

Second, it seems to be some sort of instinct to preserve the human race—it's like we evolved to not look too closely at the realities of pregnancy and childbirth. People don't want to hear that pregnancy and childbirth can be so awful, because if we were honest about how difficult it is, and how it will permanently change your body, perhaps fewer women would be willing to endure it.

When discussing pregnancy and childbirth, it's good to remember that 1) it's easy to trivialize the risks you want others to take—risks that you won't be experiencing yourself, and 2) because pregnancy and childbirth are so common, it's easy to brush them off as a minor nine-month inconvenience (topped off with a bit of pushing), when they are so much more.

THE REALITIES AND BURDENS OF PARENTING ARE UN-FATHOMABLE.

The challenges inherent in parenting are so numerous I could fill a thousand pages describing them. These challenges are never acknowledged by those who insist women should simply endure unwanted pregnancies.

Raising the next generation of healthy and happy kids has always been a huge amount of work, and even as we make progress, we continue to make motherhood harder.

Despite multiple waves of feminism, the work of raising kids in the United States is still largely a burden that falls on women. And being a mother is hard. Even in two-parent households, 70 percent of women report that they are fully or mostly responsible for housework, and 66 percent report they are fully or mostly responsible for childcare (I couldn't find a percentage for the mental/emotional work of managing a family, but feel free to estimate). Additionally, a huge number of women are the sole providers for their children—according to the Pew Research Center, mothers are the sole or primary provider in 40 percent of households with children. And even when financial support is available, it's just one factor in the mountain of tasks that are required to raise children.

There are skills that must be learned—how to bathe a child, how to change a diaper, how to potty train, how to prepare healthy food. There are endless tasks—grocery shopping, laundry, meeting emotional needs, the child's education, making sure the child gets enough sleep, food, and exercise. There are disruptions to schedules and derailing of careers. Just the amount of paperwork required for children is hard to comprehend—birth certificates, Social Security number applications, medical history forms, vaccination records, school applications, social invitations, bills to pay to keep everything running . . . the paperwork alone never ends.

And it's assumed mothers will get all these other things done (errands, paperwork, dinner prep, housework, etc.) while taking care of their child. But taking care of the child is an ongoing task itself. Women shouldn't be expected to "get stuff done" while caring for their child. Caring for their child *is already the thing they are getting done.*

It's a 24-hour-a-day occupation. There are no vacation days or sick days or paid time off from motherhood. And you can't retire from the job until you die.

There's a classic real-life story about our unwillingness to grapple with the realities of parenthood when discussing unwanted pregnancies.

One February, a woman named Jamie Jeffries was feeling proud of herself for talking a woman into continuing an unwanted pregnancy instead of getting an abortion. Eventually the baby was born, and unfortunately, six months later, for the baby's safety, the government removed the baby from the family's custody. Jamie found out about this because the mother of the baby had listed Jamie as the "preferred placement" for this baby.

Jamie was shocked and upset that someone would expect her to care for the child. She responded, "No. No no no no no no no no no! I do way too much for this work already, a six-month-old will break me, destroy my marriage and physical health. I just can't!!"

These are all legitimate reasons for why a woman might want to end an unwanted pregnancy in the first place. Motherhood is hard, and demanding it for others, while being unwilling to do it yourself, is not okay.

The United States in particular is a difficult place to be a mother. It has inaccessible, expensive healthcare; no paid leave from work; crumbling infrastructure (including public schools); and little by way of a social safety net when things go wrong. Every attempt to improve our policies is met with resistance. Instead, women are fed messages that all will be okay if we just dig in a little harder, give up some sleep, get an extra job, and sacrifice for the greater good—while also looking totally gorgeous, obviously.

And yes, I understand there are lots of fathers and other secondary caregivers who contribute substantial time, energy, and resources to parenting. Still, it is an unfathomable amount of work to raise a child.

The thing is, I could attempt an exhaustive list of *every* parenting task and every financial cost, and it would fill dozens of notebooks—and yet, it wouldn't capture what it means to be a parent, to be responsible for an entirely separate human being. I keep using this word because it fits: The existential and emotional burden of being a parent is *unfathomable*.

NO. 21

PREGNANCY SHOULD NOT BE A PUNISH- MENT.

One recurring argument leveled by people who are anti-abortion is that pregnancy is the punishment for a woman who has sex for fun instead of for reproduction. The concern is that if she's impregnated and then has an abortion, she's "getting off scot-free."

Casual suggestions that women need to become mothers, that women who don't want to be pregnant just need to deal with having a baby, that lifelong parenting responsibilities are an appropriate "consequence" or "punishment" for a women who had sex are actually bonkers.

About 60 percent of women who have abortions are already parents—so if having a baby and parenting that baby is "punishment" then they are already being punished. But also, no child should exist as a punishment! Every child deserves to be wanted and anticipated.

This should be obvious—being wanted literally helps children thrive. And it's not just that, research is clear that outcomes for children who are born from unwanted pregnancies are . . . not great. Children born from unwanted pregnancies can experience a lack of attachment with their mothers, delayed cognitive and emotional development, and a higher likelihood of experiencing domestic violence.

Beyond that, pregnancy-as-punishment doesn't make sense. Consider that women's bodies spontaneously abort 40 to 60 percent of embryos between fertilization and birth—these are called miscarriages if they occur before twenty weeks of pregnancy, and they are called stillbirths if they happen after twenty weeks. If a man impregnates a woman, then what happens if her body miscarries? Does she need to be re-impregnated in order to finish out the punishment?

The whole idea of pregnancy as punishment is nonsense.

ADOPTION IS NOT AN ALTERNATIVE TO ABORTION.

Let's start with this: The vast majority of those interested in relinquishing their child through adoption *never seriously consider abortion*. And for those who are denied access to abortion, 91 percent still won't choose adoption. Related, the adoption rate today for people denied abortion is the same as the pre-*Roe* rate.

People ask: Instead of getting an abortion, have you considered adoption? As if these are two comparable options. But based on these statistics, pregnant people see these options as unrelated, not as alternatives to each other.

Adoption is held up as an "easy fix" for abortion. You were impregnated and don't want to have the baby? Simply sacrifice your life for nine months, go through the grueling process of childbirth, and you can smoothly do the heroic act of "giving up" the child for adoption. Agencies will handle all the details so there are no complications for you or the child. Once you relinquish the child, it's a clean slate for you and a clean slate for the child. A classic win-win.

As a culture, we're beginning to understand that this narrative is deeply flawed. Adoption is rarely a clean slate for anyone involved. The actual narrative includes well-documented, widespread issues in the "adoption industry"—corruption, trauma, human-trafficking—which can bring lifelong negative repercussions for the child and the birth mother.

And yet, support for adoption is a bipartisan, unifying issue in the United States. And virtually all our media depictions point to adoption as an act of kindness and love. We choose not to challenge this narrative because it's comforting to think of adoption as a social good. It's difficult to face hard truths that we're all implicated in—and everyone's implicated, because everyone's lives are touched by adoption.

Though it's not commonly talked about, one of the biggest reasons pregnant women aren't interested in adoption is because relinquishing a baby can be a very traumatic experience. In Ann Fessler's book *The Girls Who Went Away: The Hidden History of Women Who Surrendered Children for Adoption in the Decades Before Roe v. Wade*, women describe worrying every single day of their lives about the baby they were pressured/forced to relinquish and never feeling relief about the experience. One woman who had relinquished a child and then later had an abortion said that people who claim that abortion trauma is anywhere near as bad as the trauma of relinquishment have no idea what they are talking about.

Relinquishment is not just traumatic for the mother. There's a growing body of research showing that it means lifelong trauma for the child as well. And this should be obvious to us when we consider that most adoptees in the United States don't have their original birth certificates. It's true. A legal adoption changes a baby's birth certificate and legally severs the child from their birth family. It doesn't just sever the child from their birth mother, it also severs the child from their birth father, their aunts and uncles, grandparents, and cousins on both sides of the family, their whole family tree and DNA links.

Adults who were adopted as babies have created a movement to bring awareness to the trauma of adoption. Some didn't find out they were adopted until they became adults, and the revelation shook the very foundations of their existence. Some were adopted from another culture and denied a chance to learn about that culture—leaving them feeling out of place in any culture. Some know they were adopted and fear accidentally dating someone they share DNA with. Some experience anxiety not knowing the medical history of their birth families and what sorts of medical issues they might face. Some take DNA tests as adults and receive the emotional news that they have half or full siblings they never knew about.

Adoption does not always have the storybook ending we've been sold. It should not be approached casually or lightly, and whenever possible, all efforts to keep the baby with its birth parents should be the priority. Adoption should not be looked at as an easy fix for an unwanted pregnancy.

THERE ARE ZERO CONSEQUENCES FOR MEN WHO EJACULATE IRRESPONSIBLY.

If a man ejaculates irresponsibly and causes an unwanted pregnancy, he faces zero consequences. He can walk away at any time, and our current culture doesn't really do much (or anything?) to discourage it.

If the woman wants to take Plan B to prevent a pregnancy, it's on the woman to procure it and pay for it (from her own funds, or by asking for money from someone else).

If the woman decides to have an abortion, the man may never know he caused an unwanted pregnancy with his irresponsible ejaculation—and it's still on the woman to make arrangements and pay to get one (again, from her own funds, or by asking for money from someone else—and that's assuming she can get herself to a state where it is legal).

If the woman decides to raise the baby but doesn't tell the man, or relinquishes the baby for adoption, he may never know that there's now a child walking around with 50 percent of his DNA.

If the woman does tell the man that he caused an unwanted pregnancy and that she's having the baby, the closest thing to a consequence for him is that he *may* need to pay child support. But our current child support system is well known to be a joke.

Men make up 85 percent of child support providers, and only 43.5 percent of parents report receiving the full amount of child support due. And an estimated $10 billion in child support payments go uncollected each year. In cases where men won't pay to support a child, theoretically, women have legal recourse and can force a man to pay child support, but, again, the system makes it extremely hard. It is up to the mother to pay to prove paternity, pay a lawyer, and fight for child support in court.

Keep in mind these court battles are unreasonably hard to manage for someone who just had a baby—a baby whom they are trying to feed and care for. And ultimately, even if she puts in the time and pays the years of legal fees, most women never collect all the money anyway. If she does manage to collect, the average child support order is $400 a month, which is obviously not even close to what it takes to house and clothe and feed and educate a child—to say nothing about the temporal, emotional, and physical costs of raising a child.

Our society is set up to protect men from the consequences of their own actions. Our laws and policies could not be better designed to protect men who abandon the pregnancies they cause.

I had a conversation with a long-time social worker about this, and she listed eight ways that men face no consequences and are not held responsible for their ejaculatory actions.

1) There are no laws that require the father to pay child support without a court order. It's not automatic.

2) In many states, credit scores are not affected by failure to pay child support.

3) Fathers aren't fired from their jobs for impregnating a woman.

4) Fathers are not billed for any medical expenses for the pregnancy or the child. (In at least two states, fathers can be legally required to pay for at least 50 percent of pregnancy related medical costs. Should we assume the mother has to be willing to fight for those payments—via paperwork and dealing with state agencies—from unwilling fathers?)

5) Fathers don't have to take unpaid weeks or months off work for pregnancy complications or childbirth.

6) Fathers don't lose a cent in wages for impregnating a woman.

7) Fathers aren't generally required to pay any funeral expenses for a deceased child. (At least two states consider it the responsibility of both parents to pay.)

8) If fathers choose to walk out at any point (before or after the child is born), there are no societal consequences for abandoning the child.

There are little to no repercussions for skipping out. So, many men keep going along, causing unwanted pregnancies with irresponsible ejaculations and never giving it a thought. When the topic of abortion comes up, they might think: *Abortion makes me uncomfortable. Women should not choose abortion.* And they never once consider the man who *caused* the unwanted pregnancy.

Note No. 1

We could argue there are significant societal consequences for men who abandon their children. The assumption is that such a man would be castigated and shunned. But there is no way of knowing a man has abandoned a child unless he (or someone who knows his past community) volunteers the information.

Note No. 2

What would it look like if there were real and immediate consequences for men who cause an unwanted pregnancy? What kind of consequences would make sense? Should they be financial? A loss of rights or freedoms? Should they be as harsh, painful, nauseating, scarring, expensive, risky, and life-altering as forcing a woman to go through a nine-month unwanted pregnancy?

Let's imagine what it would be like to legislate men's bodies instead of women's bodies. Pretend that at the onset of puberty, all males in the United States are required by law to bank their sperm and then get a vasectomy. If/when the male becomes a responsible adult, and perhaps finds a mate, if they want to have a baby, they can use the banked sperm, or if necessary, the vasectomy can be reversed, and then redone once the childbearing stage is over. This would certainly eliminate essentially all unwanted pregnancies, so it seems like it would be welcome legislation for anyone who is serious about wanting to reduce abortion.

Or perhaps you are having trouble wrapping your head around the idea of physical consequences for men? Even about though we seem to be more than fine with physical consequences for women? That sounds like something we as a society should address.

SPERM ARE DANGEROUS.

Sperm should be considered a dangerous bodily fluid that can cause pain, a lifetime of disruption, and even death for some. Sperm can create a person. Sperm can kill a person. Sperm cause pregnancy, and pregnancy and childbirth can result in physical and mental health issues for women, as well as negative impacts to her social status, job status, and financial status.

A man who is about to ejaculate sperm and place it in a woman's body should be acutely aware of what that sperm can do to her, and he should act accordingly, by which I mean responsibly. Every single time he has sex. The consequences are too immense to not do so.

It's especially important for men to be responsible for their own bodies and bodily fluids because:

1) Men are always fertile. They never have to guess if it's a fertile day; they know it is. They are a loaded gun at all times.

2) The man is 1,000 percent in the best position to either prevent or cause a pregnancy due to simple human physiology.

3) Condoms and vasectomies are easier, cheaper, safer, simpler, and more convenient than birth control options for women.

We need to teach men what it means to take responsibility for their fertility. We need to drill home the fact that men are fertile every single day.

Men are essentially walking around with a dangerous weapon, not a plaything. How they manage their sperm has life and death consequences. To the extent we have not underscored the grave reality of that fact, we have seriously failed men and women.

MEN
HAVE MORE
CONTROL
OF THEIR BODIES AND
SEXUAL
URGES
THAN WE LIKE
TO ADMIT.

I admit, as a woman I've never felt a man's sexual urge. I can only compare it to a woman's sexual urge (which has nothing to do with ejaculating sperm into a vagina). I know women's sexual urges are strong, but some say men's sexual urges are much stronger. How does a woman's sexual urge compare to a man's sexual urge? Well, we actually don't know.

There is no test case where we can raise a woman outside a patriarchal society, where she's not constantly told that a woman's sex drive is much weaker than a man's sex drive. Where she's not told repeatedly that women don't really enjoy sex. That it's "normal" for a woman to fake an orgasm during sex to placate a man's ego, and that it doesn't matter if she experiences pleasure during sex.

It's true I don't know the extent of men's sexual urges. But I do know bodily urges. I know urges that all humans experience that are far, far stronger than sexual urges for both men and women—the urge to urinate and defecate. They are urges so strong that even if I ignore them, my body will take over and act on those urges.

All humans know those urges, but we have learned to control them. We don't just pee anywhere. We pee in toilets. We hold it till we get there. We build bathroom breaks into our day.

We're not asking too much when we expect men to control their sexual urges, when we expect men to take responsibility for their own bodily fluids, when we expect men to ejaculate responsibly.

MEN CAN EASILY PREVENT ABORTIONS BUT CHOOSE NOT TO.

Most abortions are elective and due to unwanted pregnancy. But there are some abortions that happen during *wanted* pregnancies, and without exception they are heartbreaking. The fetus dies in utero or has medical issues that are incompatible with life or the mother has a medical issue that won't allow her body to support the pregnancy further. Again, these are heartbreaking circumstances, and thankfully they make up a very small percentage of abortions.

I point that out because men could easily prevent elective abortion, which is virtually all abortion, simply by ejaculating responsibly.

Men mostly run our government. Men mostly make the laws. For almost fifty years, a lot of men were focused on what it would take to overturn *Roe v. Wade*, claiming they wanted to reduce abortions. And then, in June 2022, the Supreme Court, made up of mostly men, *did* overturn *Roe v. Wade*.

Five decades of work. It's strange when you think about it, because if men were actually interested in reducing abortion, it didn't need to take fifty years. At any point, men could have eliminated elective abortions in a very short amount of time—a matter of weeks—without ever touching an abortion law, without legislating about women's bodies, without even mentioning women. All men had to do was ejaculate responsibly.

They chose not to.

Today, they continue to choose not to.

NO. 27

WE KNOW WHAT WORKS.

I don't know if this is your goal, but if you want to reduce the number of abortions in our country, both in states where abortion is legal and states where abortion is illegal, I have very good news for you. We know how to do it. We have good data on what reduces abortions, and it's not magic.

The most effective, proven way to reduce abortions that we know of is free and accessible birth control. An ounce of prevention is worth a pound of cure.

We know that in countries where birth control is affordable or free and more easily available to anyone who wants it, there are much lower rates of unwanted pregnancy. In fact, currently, the rate of unwanted pregnancy in the United States is 21 percent higher than the average in other Western countries.

But it's not just something that happens to work in other countries and won't work in the United States. We've tried it here and we know it works. Colorado created a program that made birth control free and easily accessible. The result? Abortion rates fell by almost half. And not just Colorado—St. Louis had a similar program with great results. As a bonus, these programs can save millions of dollars. The health department in Colorado reported that every dollar spent on that birth control initiative saved $5.85 for Colorado's Medicaid program.

In addition to free and accessible birth control, good sex education is also a really effective way to reduce abortions. We see this in The Netherlands, where teenage girls have a pregnancy rate that is four times lower than teen girls in the United States. Dutch teens also have much lower rates of sexually transmitted infections.

The biggest reason for the low numbers in The Netherlands is that the country mandates comprehensive sex education for all students. Kids receive age-appropriate sex ed in every grade. The information they receive is medically accurate, and they can ask questions and get honest responses.

That's not how sex education works in the United States, where every state can take a different approach. At the moment, some states allow sex education, but only with a focus on abstinence. Other states allow sex education, but only specific information is allowed to be shared, and teachers can only respond to questions that fall within the specific approved curriculum. And there are eleven states that don't require any sex education at all.

It's wonderful that data about how to reduce abortions is available and that it's clear what has been successful. Even more hopeful, these efforts (free birth control, high-quality sex education) have been made in an environment that hasn't seriously considered irresponsible ejaculations as *the singular cause* of unwanted pregnancies.

A culture of ejaculating responsibly, combined with free and accessible birth control and thorough sex education, will bring the number of unwanted pregnancies close to zero.

Note No. 1

Some might assume that abortions will end in the United States because *Roe v. Wade* was overturned. There is no data to support that. In countries with full abortion bans, research shows that up to 68 percent of unwanted pregnancies are still aborted.

Overturning *Roe v. Wade* did not create a full abortion ban, and some of the most populous states in the country still allow abortion, which would lead us to predict that the 68 percent statistic will be even higher in the United States. Experts believe the availability of abortion pills delivered via federal mail will also enable abortions to continue in private homes, even in states where abortion is banned.

Since abortion bans have been shown to be ineffective, shifting the focus to preventing unwanted pregnancies is a much more sensible and impactful path to reducing abortions.

THIS IS HOW TO TAKE ACTION.

We need to change things. Women's lives are literally on the line here. *Roe v. Wade* has been overturned. Women in the United States being forced to continue unwanted pregnancies is no longer theoretical. We have an urgent need to change the discourse, and we need practical ideas that focus on preventing unwanted pregnancies.

I've discussed the arguments in this book with thousands of people over several years. From the responses I have witnessed to these ideas, I know that people can change and that the discourse can change. They can change quickly and profoundly. The information is new to many people, and some resist it, but the majority take it in as new and better knowledge, and they approach future sexual encounters more responsibly.

START WHERE YOU ARE

Men, commit to ejaculate responsibly yourself and build a culture that expects all men to ejaculate responsibly.

Insist on a condom every time you have sex. Experiment until you find a condom that works really well for you and your partner so that you don't ever feel like it's a bummer when you use a condom. Keep your favorite condoms stocked in your nightstand. Keep some in your glovebox or backpack. Buy your favorites to keep at your partner's house.

If you've figured out condom and lubrication methods that work well, share what you've learned so others can benefit.

Make an appointment for a vasectomy. If you're nervous about needing a reversal in the future, bank your sperm first.

If you've already had a vasectomy, talk openly to other men and women about how wonderful it is, how it lifts a huge stress that hangs over sexual encounters.

If you hear anyone joking or talking negatively about condoms or vasectomies, say something like:

- *But, actually, condoms are awesome. So much safer. I don't want an STI or to get anyone pregnant.*

- *I know we joke about this, but I would never, ever, ever have unprotected sex unless we were both fully on board with trying to conceive.*

- *Once I learned how to use condoms correctly, I never looked back.*

- *Sex-is-bad-with-condoms is such a myth.*

CHANGE THE DISCOURSE

Through demonstrating and talking about responsible personal behavior, we can normalize condom use so much that asking "Should I wear a condom?" is universally recognized as a ridiculous question. Just like asking "Should I wear a seatbelt?" is ridiculous.

If people don't like the shift in conversation from women's bodies to men's bodies, call them out. Say: *I don't get why a person would argue about holding men responsible for their actions, especially if it reduced unwanted pregnancies in a major way.*

If people try to distract from the central, practical issues, keep returning the conversation to pregnancy prevention and irresponsible ejaculations.

Don't lecture women about their bodies while avoiding conversations with men about their bodies.

These conversations can shift the national and worldwide conversation around abortion away from unproductive debates about women's bodies and toward helpful and practical discussions about what men can do to prevent pregnancy.

DEMAND FACT-BASED SEX EDUCATION

We need to create a movement that makes sex education a priority. We need to demand thorough sex-ed at multiple points in K–12 education.

We need a curriculum with clear descriptions about the differences in fertility between men and women and the implications these have for preventing unwanted pregnancy.

We need a curriculum that clearly specifies that sperm cause pregnancy and makes ejaculating responsibly the clear, universal expectation.

We need a curriculum that educates men on how to use a condom effectively and dispels the view that sex with a condom is not pleasurable.

We need to normalize healthy, responsible behaviors, attitudes, and conversations about men managing where to deposit sperm. Sex education needs to make it unmistakably clear that men can ejaculate almost anywhere but in a woman's vagina.

We need to teach all the different types of birth control options for men and women, their pros and cons, and what options might work best in different phases of life. We need to actively fight any stigma against condoms and vasectomies.

We need to point out and break down the cultural expectations and problematic power dynamics around birth control and sex.

We need to give young people the full spectrum of information—the good and the bad—about pregnancy, childbirth, and parenting, and allow them to make informed choices. We need to make clear that there is no easy, risk-free way to have a baby.

INCREASE ACCESS TO BIRTH CONTROL

Since we know birth control programs work, we need to make birth control as accessible as possible.

We can make condoms even more accessible.

We can fund new birth control options for men. (The results of the study on birth control for men discussed in argument 10 were very promising. What else can we explore along these lines?)

We can create a demand for more doctors to be trained in the latest vasectomy and vasectomy reversal techniques, so we can achieve high success rates for those who want them.

We can make oral contraceptives over the counter—like they are in a hundred different countries—and we can fight to make a wide variety of contraceptives free in every state.

We can improve pain prevention protocols for IUD insertion and removal to make them a more attractive option for more people.

HOLD POLITICIANS ACCOUNTABLE

Refuse to let politicians and political groups grand-stand about abortion. Be clear that if they are focusing on women, or celebrating an ineffective ban, then they are wasting everybody's time. If they actually care about reducing or eliminating the number of abortions in our country, they need to show how they plan to prevent unwanted pregnancies and hold men responsible for their actions.

In every Q&A with a politician and every political debate where abortion is brought up, ask specific questions: *What is your plan for preventing irresponsible ejaculations? Where are the programs for free, accessible birth control? Where are the statewide sex-ed programs that explain how dangerous sperm is? What should the legal consequences be for men who cause unwanted pregnancies?*

Call politicians out for hypocrisy, for using abortion as a political tool. Don't let them derail the conversation with emotional appeals. Force them to answer questions about actual steps they are taking that are proven to reduce unwanted pregnancies and irresponsible ejaculations.

Since I first shared some of the ideas in this book, we've seen the conversations start to shift. We've seen people waking up to and embracing the fact that men cause pregnancy and that they can most easily prevent pregnancy. People are seeing the futility of a focus on abortion, the nonsense and hypocrisy of slut-shaming, and the immoral efforts to regulate and control women's bodies, when instead, everything can be resolved with a singular focus:

Ejaculate responsibly.

NOTE

Thank you for reading *Ejaculate Responsibly*.

I share so many facts and statistics and reports in this book. If you'd like to look them up to verify information or to learn more, you're in luck, because I have sources for everything. This book was thoroughly and deeply fact-checked, and the end notes for this little volume are almost as long as the book itself. (I'm exaggerating, but not as much as you might think.)

I'm putting all the sources and overly complicated urls at this easy link:

workman.com/EjaculateResponsibly

If you want to share your thoughts, tag me @designmom on Twitter or Instagram. I look forward to retweeting or interacting with your ideas.

ACKNOWLEDGMENTS

It's a little book, but there are many people who helped to make it better, and I want to thank them.

First there's my husband and partner of twenty-seven years, Ben Blair, who is my favorite person. He has been my biggest cheerleader through this entire process. He did a careful read using his Philosophy Professor skills, making thorough notes to help me structure arguments and say what I needed to say. I'll forever remember the long evening spent together as the book was nearing completion, and I was just tweaking words here and there; he read each page aloud so that I could hear if anything was hard to read or just not flowing well, and he took breaks every few pages to say kind things to me.

I want to thank my children, Ralph, Maude, Olive, Oscar, Betty, and Flora June. Ralph was twenty years old when I started sharing the ideas in this book. Flora June was nine years old. At that time they had no idea how often their mother would be talking about very specific aspects about the causes of unwanted pregnancies on very public platforms. It's a reminder that kids don't get to choose their parents, and sometimes their parents might write about irresponsible ejaculations. Over the past few years, strangers and acquaintances, and even relatives, have demanded that my kids debate them about something I've written, which is not fair to my kids, and not something they signed up for. And I'm sorry I don't know how to protect them better from this sort of thing. I'm grateful for the patience of my children. I'm grateful for their enthusiasm every time I shared a cover design or new edit. And I'm grateful they make protest signs that say EJACULATE RESPONSIBLY and I ♥ VASECTOMIES.

Thank you to my agent, Meg Thompson, who made sure to get this book into the hands of the right publisher. Meg listens well, she has my back, and she's so good at sending calming emails when I need them.

Thank you to my publisher, Lia Ronnen, who treated this book as not only publishable, but as vital and urgent. My first phone call with Lia about the possibility of writing my first book, *Design Mom*, was twelve years ago. This book is about as different from that one as any two books could be. I can hardly believe my good fortune of having Lia come into my life when I was still figuring out my voice. She has pushed me to write more and better, and she has had a vision for my books before I have.

Thank you to fine folks at Workman Publishing. To Maisie Tivnan for editing, which is really a fancy word for helping me to think better. To Kim Daly and Claudia Sorsby, the copy editor and fact checker, for helping me get things right. To Barbara Peragine and Janet Vicario who did the type and layout work and indulged my opinions. Thanks to the marketing team, Rebecca Carlisle, Moira Kerrigan, Claire Gross, and Terri Ruffino. There are lots of other hands at Workman that this book passed through and who helped bring it to the world; I haven't met them and don't know their names, but I'm grateful for them.

Thank you to the legendary Bonnie Siegler who created the design for this book—both the cover and the interior. It was a pleasure and a distinct honor to work with her. Her passion for this work and care for the design of the book that matched my care for the arguments is a gift I couldn't have hoped for.

Thank you to Laurie Smithwick who consulted on design and gave me a history lesson on the Avant Garde font.

Thank you to my friend Diana M. Hartman who helped me clarify and expand my arguments. Diana's dedication to sharing these ideas and her patience in countless back-and-forths with people who presented nonstop sexist nonsense kept the ideas alive when I was exhausted.

Thank you to Laura Mayes who makes time to talk through my current projects and point me in the most productive direction.

Thank you to my siblings who share my work, defend me, and support me. Before I told the world about this book, I texted a link to my siblings, and each one replied with a pre-order receipt.

Thank you to my mom who has been a constant giver of confidence throughout my entire life. She isn't always comfortable with the things I write, but she loves me anyway.

Thank you to Samantha Bee and Dr. Jennifer Gunter for introducing me to the term "penile winter."

Lastly, I want to thank Twitter—both the platform and the people who use it. Not everyone loves Twitter, but I experience it as an incredible place to learn. I've had my prejudices broken down. I've had my outlook expanded. I've encountered important points of view that would not have reached me via my real life community. I've discussed and debated all sorts of topics on Twitter almost daily for four years. It's been an exercise in making my writing and thinking clearer and more resonant. And I'm grateful for it.

THE ARGUMENTS

Gabrielle Blair is the founder of DesignMom.com. Started in 2006, it has been named a Website of the Year by *Time* magazine, praised as a top parenting blog by *The Wall Street Journal*, *Parents*, and *Better Homes and Gardens*, and won the Iris Award for Blog of the Year. Her first book, *Design Mom: How to Live with Kids*, a *New York Times* bestseller, was published in 2015 by Artisan. Gabrielle is also a founder of Alt Summit, the blockbuster annual conference for online content creators and creative entrepreneurs, currently in its thirteenth year.

As a thought leader for more than fifteen years, Gabrielle has written and moderated hundreds of discussions on difficult topics and interviewed some of the most influential people in the world. Her writing is quoted and shared across the globe daily. Gabrielle and her husband, Ben Blair, have six children—Ralph, Maude, Olive, Oscar, Betty, and Flora June. After six years in Oakland, California, they now live in Normandy, France. You can follow Gabrielle on Instagram and Twitter at @DesignMom.